MW01615718

God's Plan for Peace in the Middle East

Rev. Dr. Douglas W. Kittredge

Copyright © 2006 by Douglas W. Kittredge

All rights reserved. No part of this book shall be reproduced or transmitted in any form or by any means, electronic, mechanical, magnetic, photographic including photocopying, recording or by any information storage and retrieval system, without prior written permission of the publisher. No patent liability is assumed with respect to the use of the information contained herein. Although every precaution has been taken in the preparation of this book, the publisher and author assume no responsibility for errors or omissions. Neither is any liability assumed for damages resulting from the use of the information contained herein.

ISBN 0-7414-2842-3

Published by:

INFINITY
PUBLISHING.COM

1094 New DeHaven Street, Suite 100
West Conshohocken, PA 19428-2713
Info@buybooksontheweb.com
www.buybooksontheweb.com
Toll-free (877) BUY BOOK
Local Phone (610) 941-9999
Fax (610) 941-9959

Printed in the United States of America

Printed on Recycled Paper

Published May 2007

CONTENTS

Acknowledgments

Our world has changed from a world of hope into one of continued anxiety because of the threat of terror. The living God is a God of hope who is sovereign over the turmoil in the world and offers us great hope for the future. *"In the world you will have tribulation, but be of good cheer, I have overcome the world"* (John 16:33). God's Word is a continual joy and I am thankful that no matter how dark the shadows of the days to come, our God will sustain us by the hope He gives us in the gospel.

I am deeply grateful to a significant number who have shared the excitement and hope expressed in this book:

- To Jim Melnick, a faithful friend, brother, and pilgrim in this world and a fellow traveler on numerous trips to Israel. Jim has encouraged and stimulated the audacious vision expressed in this book. He urged me to put my thoughts into writing and has always enthusiastically supported the feeblest of my efforts to express my dreams.

- To Sean Whitenack and Sam Capitano, co-laborers as elders in New Life in Christ Church who painstakingly edited my initial manuscripts. I am very grateful for their interest and support in this effort.

- To Christine Fulcrod for her repeated typing and retyping of the manuscript from handwritten yellow pages. She has taken the project on with great enthusiasm and has carefully worked out the details with the publisher for a first-time author.

- To the pastors in Israel who have permitted me to share in their lives and the lives of their congregations in order to gain a better understanding of their needs and concerns.

- To the congregation of New Life in Christ Church for their sharing their vision, supporting enthusiastically our ministry and rejoicing in the greatness and grandeur of our holy God whose glory extends throughout history and our world.

- To my family who have shared my dreams and who have helped shape my thoughts by encouragement and questions that have sharpened by expression of the vision.

- To my wife who has listened for years to my dreams for the salvation of Jews and Palestinian Arabs and has always encouraged me in my vision. She, too, has made pilgrimages to Israel to do what we urge others to do in this book.

May the Lord be glorified in the ministry of this book. May the Lord call many to Himself for His own glory.

Foreword

Since the destruction of the Temple in Jerusalem in 70 AD by the Romans and the subsequent Diaspora, the Jewish people have, essentially, been "on the run." Scattered throughout the world in the intervening centuries, they have often suffered horrible persecutions, from the Inquisition in Spain to the pogroms in Russia's Pale of Settlement to the Holocaust of Nazi Germany. Even in those nations where Jews started to feel at ease, they have never truly been at ease. Among the Orthodox and ultra-Orthodox there has been the constant longing for the coming of Messiah ("Moshiach," the Anointed One promised in Scripture). Among secular Jews – so many of whom have turned their backs on the God of Abraham, Isaac and Jacob – there is still this sense among many that the Jewish people have been empowered or given a trust to do something – *"tikkun olam"* is one concept expressing this in Hebrew - the goal of "fixing up or repairing the world," but they don't quite know how to do it. They know that the world is broken and that they should do something to try to fix it. Thus, many Jewish people engage in "mitzvot" ("good deeds," literally, "the commandments"). This is the view that doing good deeds – donating a wing of a hospital or helping the poor and disadvantaged – is the essence of fulfilling the commandments.

Orthodox Jews have a similar view but believe they must also follow the literal commandments of the Tenakh (the Hebrew Scriptures, or, the Old Testament to Christians) in order to please God. Of these commandments, there are not just the Ten Commandments that are well-known to the world (or maybe not so well-known anymore?), but 613. These 613 commandments must be fulfilled according to the strictures of the Talmud and other Jewish commentaries, according to the Orthodox view. Some of these commandments can no longer be practiced, since they depended on Temple worship in Jerusalem and the Jewish Temple no longer exists.

Enter the creation of the State of Israel in 1948. In that year the ancient Jewish homeland and the Temple Mount itself once again came under Jewish control for the first time since they were lost to the Romans in 70 AD. This event has had the whole world in an uproar since that time. We are reminded of the prophet Zechariah (2:2-3) when he speaks about Jerusalem becoming a "heavy stone" with the nations of the world gathered against her.

Some passionately support the Jews' right to their ancestral lands; others, such as Muslim terrorists, violently oppose it with every fiber of their being – some blowing themselves up in suicide bombings against the Jews and those who support them. There is even the Al Aqsa Martyrs' Brigade, an Islamic terrorist group named for one of the two mosques on the Temple Mount. America saw this terrorist hatred vividly played out in full horror during the terrorist attacks on the United States on September 11, 2001.

The Promise – No "Un-Choosing!"

It cannot be said that the world is in any way "settled" on the issue of whether the Jews should have their place in "Zion," that is, the Land of Israel, or more specifically, the "City of Zion" itself, Jerusalem. The religious or political view that the Jewish people deserve this place and are to be left in peace is commonly referred to as "Zionism."

One thing is for sure – the Scriptures make clear that the Jewish people will not be left "in peace" until certain events occur, though the desire of their hearts – both the secular and the ultra-religious - is simply to be left alone by the rest of the world. This brings to mind Tevye the milkman's plea to God in the play "Fiddler on the Roof": "I know, I know," he says, looking up to Heaven, that "we are

8

your Chosen People. But once in a while, can't You choose someone else?" We might smile at Tevye's question, but the answer is no – and also, yes! God cannot "un-choose" the Jewish people. He is a covenant God Who remains true to His promises even when men and women are unfaithful. Rather than "un-choosing" the Jewish people, He has enlarged the Tent. His promise of salvation is now available to all who come to Him in faith, Jew or Gentile. In the Book of Isaiah God the Father says to His Son: "'It is too small a thing that You should be My Servant to raise up the tribes of Jacob and to restore the preserved ones of Israel; I will also make you a light of the nations so that My salvation may reach to the end of the earth." (Isaiah 49:6)

All who come to Him must come by faith in the Messiah through repentance and by accepting His free gift of grace. There is no "dual-track" where the Jewish people are saved just because they are Jewish. That is a notion floating around in some circles but is complete heresy.

God will remain faithful to His covenant promises made to the Jewish patriarchs and the Children of Israel. He will do so because that is His character. The Word of God says, *"Behold, I have inscribed you on the palms of my hands"* (Isaiah 49:16). God will continue pursuing the Jewish people because those who will be redeemed from among them are destined to be a praise in the whole earth, worshipping their Messiah and the Savior of the world, beginning from Jerusalem. All the peoples of the earth will see the greatness of God and His glory through how He deals with this most intractable of issues, the fate of the Jewish people, whom no one - Pharaoh, the Tsars, the Inquisitors, Hitler, Stalin, or a host of others – has been able to destroy.

The promise of Romans 11 in the Brit Chadashah (the New Covenant or New Testament), where the Apostle Paul speaks of this coming day or event, is that it will be one unlike anything in the history of the world since the Resurrection itself. He writes: "For if their rejection [that is, the Jews' rejection of Messiah Jesus] be the reconciliation of the world, what will their acceptance be but life from the dead?" (11:13)

Gog and Magog

On a recent visit to Jerusalem, I happened upon a poster in a bookstore in the Jewish Quarter of the Old City. It showed a view of the Temple Mount after the invasion of Gog and Magog, the enemies of Israel depicted by the prophet Ezekiel in chapters 38 and 39. The poster showed the Temple Mount in two phases, "Before Gog" and "After Gog." The first shot showed the Temple Mount as presently constituted. The second view showed the Temple Mount without the Dome of the Rock and Al Aqsa mosques and in the place of the former was the Third Jewish Temple. The implications were quite clear.

I served for many years as a Russian affairs analyst in the Pentagon during the height of the Cold War and its aftermath. I have also been involved in Jewish evangelical ministry – mostly to Russian Jews - for almost three decades. I am well familiar with the prophecy of Gog and Magog from nearly every perspective. If future events transpire as depicted on that poster, they will indeed shake the world politically and militarily to its very foundations.

In our generation many have believed that the former Soviet Union and its Arab allies were the Gog and Magog of Ezekiel's prophecy, that these nations would invade Israel, where their armies would be destroyed. That interpretation seemed to fit world events at the time, and it may still do so, although in a different form, since the Soviet Union is no more. Perhaps something along the lines of an invasion of Israel by Russia and Muslim allies will still occur or perhaps it will be something else entirely - we do not know precisely how the events of the "end times" will unfold; we only know that the Lord will return, His people shall be victorious, and all who love Him and are redeemed shall be with Him forever.

The point, though, is that students of prophecy can speculate endlessly on the events, nations and times of the future – whether it is the prophecy about Gog and Magog or others. The shelves of our Christian bookstores are filled with such books, while there are innumerable conferences, messages and tapes on similar subjects. These might or might not be edifying to the people involved, depending on how they are used. The question is, are they being used to build the Kingdom of God or only to speculate on the future? This is not to criticize all books on prophecy – only to say that, very often, the perspective is out of joint. Like many things in our society today, much of it seems "me-driven," even for the believer, as in, 'What good things will happen to *me*' in the future? 'What terrible things will happen to *them*?' That spirit is not the spirit of godliness or the heart of missions.

However, the pursuit of prophecy that is directed toward the building up of God's Kingdom – and not just speculating over what the Bible says will happen next – reflects a mature faith. The prophecy of Romans 11, which deals with the ultimate salvation of the remnant of the Jewish people, is such a passage. This prophecy, in fact, plays a key role in the unfolding of God's plan and His Kingdom, yet one will find relatively little written about it on our bookshelves today. It has been crowded out. One could speculate on the reasons why, but I will leave that to the reader.

The Puritan Hope

It was not always so. Many of the great Puritan Reformers, for example, wrote and meditated on this prophecy a great deal. There were differences of views then as now, but many amazing statements stand out as clarion calls through the centuries. Many of these are captured in the excellent volume of scholarship called *The Puritan Hope* by Iain H. Murray, published by the Banner of Truth Trust in 1991. There is Samuel Rutherford (for whom the present-day

Rutherford Institute is named). In 1635 he wrote: "O to see the sight, next to Christ's coming in the clouds, the most joyful! Our elder brethren the Jews and Christ fall upon one another's necks and kiss each other! They have long been asunder.... O longed-for and lovely day-dawn! O sweet Jesus, let me see that sight which will be as life from the dead, thee and thy ancient people in mutual embraces." (Murray, p. 98). Thomas Boston of the Church of Scotland, preaching in 1716, said these words, "Have you any love to, or concern for the Church, for the work of reformation, the reformation of our country, the reformation of the world? Any longing desire for the revival of the work now at a stand; for a flourishing state of the church, that is now under a decay? Then pray for the conversion of the Jews." (Murray, p. 113). There are many, many more, but, finally, I will cite one of the greatest of all American preachers, Jonathan Edwards: "Nothing is more certainly foretold than this national conversion of the Jews in Romans 11."

"The Dream"

This book is about the great prophecy of Romans 11. It is about a Dream. An original title was "We Are Like Dreamers," reminding us of the great passage in Psalm 126: "When the Lord brought back the captive ones from Zion, we were like those who dream." (Psalm 126:1). Dr. Doug Kittredge is my brother in Messiah, friend, pastor and co-laborer in ministry. It is this Dream that we and many others are committed to because it is promised in God's Word. Though none of us knows exactly how it will occur, we know that it will indeed come to pass. It was this Dream, in part, that led four of us to found the Israel Theological Seminary in 2003. I am privileged to serve with him and to help prepare in some small way for the fulfillment of this Dream. What a joy it is to see his love for our Lord and for Israel to know his pastor's heart! What a humbling and moving experience it has been for us to go to the Western Wall together to pray for the peace of Jerusalem and for the salvation of the Jewish people and to see the hand of God leading us and many others to be a part of this Dream!

When the Lord called my wife Karen and myself to ministry to Russian Jews in 1978, He gave us a deep love and devotion to these people who had experienced so much suffering and persecution under Communism and, in earlier generations, under the Russian Empire's Pale of Settlement that came before. In one sense they are a people group like any other that needs to be reached with the gospel. But there is more. We saw the beginnings of a major spiritual Awakening ("probuzhdeniye" in Russian) among them. God began moving among the Russian Jewish people in an astounding way. Many started coming to Him as they heard the gospel and cast aside the atheism they were taught in the former Soviet Union. They have become a sort of "first fruits" of Jewish believers in Jesus in this generation. This was a generation of people whose Jewishness was nearly completely extinguished in the former Soviet Union. Yet God preserved them as a people and has called a number of them to Himself. Is this a precursor to the fulfillment of Romans 11? Are these forerunners of the Dream? One of them was my dear friend and co-laborer Anna Portnov, who is now with the Lord. Anna understood the Dream. Some years ago she wrote: "God loves Israel but until Israel acknowledges her sin, [there] won't be peace; she won't be blessed."

Russian Jewish believers in Jesus as the Messiah now compose the largest segment of evangelical believers in Israel. They meet in *kehilat* (assemblies) and house groups throughout the country. It is my privilege with Doug and others to have a ministry of encouragement to many of these pastors and leaders in the Land of Israel.

Let me also tell you about Vladimir (or "Vlad"). Vlad is from the Jewish Autonomous Region, also known as Birobidzhan, located in the Russian Far East and set up by Stalin to re-settle the Jews. Today Vlad is a prisoner in Ukraine and is a Jewish believer in Jesus. I do not know what he is in prison for, but I believe he dearly loves the Lord. There are also other believers with him there in that prison. Vlad is begging for more Messianic literature in Russian, including our *International Messianic Newspaper*, for him and his friends and other assistance. He writes, "I just now ask you, in the name of our Lord Yeshua, don't forget and leave me, please…" We are not forgetting him. We also published the first chapter of this book in Russian in that newspaper to encourage Russian Jewish believers like Vlad, wherever they may be, and to serve as a testimony to unbelievers. Oksana, a believer in Uzbekistan, writes to ask about getting the entire book in Russian – that will be our next project, Lord willing!

As you read this book yourself, think of those whom you know, Jew and Gentile, who are not imprisoned behind bars like Vlad, yet are still in a prison of unbelief and rebellion against God. Nevertheless, Vlad can rejoice in the Lord despite his present circumstances. Please pray for him and Jewish believers in Jesus like him all around the world. Pray for the day when "all Israel will be saved…The Deliverer will come from Zion, He will remove ungodliness from Jacob, and this is My covenant with them, when I take away their sins." (Romans 11:26)

I highly commend this book to you for your careful consideration and study. This is also a way of passing the torch from previous generations. That torch is a symbol of faith in God's promises in Romans 11 and the rest of Scripture and what those promises mean – both for the priority of missions and for the future of the world.

Jim Melnick
President,
Friends of Russian Jewry, Inc.
Fredericksburg, Virginia
December, 2005

Chapter 1

Imagine

"Jerusalem is a cup of trembling in the hands of all the nations," asserts the prophet Zechariah. The muezzins' call to prayer from the Al Aqsa mosque on the Temple Mount breaks the stillness of the night at 4:15 a.m. Later what sounds like a bell concerto calls faithful monastics to matins, or morning prayers. At 9 a.m., black-hooded Armenian Orthodox priests tap rods with metal ends to clear a path for a procession from St. Stephen's Church into the alleyways of the Armenian Quarter. At the Western Wall scores of Hasidic Jewish men bind on phylacteries - leather cases holding Scripture passages - to their foreheads and arms and carefully wash their hands to approach the Western Wall.

How can a city where worshippers of God so loudly and boldly proclaim their love and zeal for Him also be a city whose citizens are engulfed in conflict and hostility? Doesn't Jerusalem mean "City of Peace"? Yet every stone has a history to tell of wars and hatreds that have existed for thousands of years down to the present day. The very air over Jerusalem hangs moist with prayers and dreams. To this day chants mix with curses, faith with fear, and hopes with confusion.

On November 29, 1947, the United Nations voted to end the British Mandate and extend statehood to Israel. At that time Jerusalem was declared to be an international city, not under the custodianship of any nation. Yet the UN had no way to enforce such a declaration. In fact Jordan controlled the city and a war broke out in Jerusalem as the Jews attempted to take control of it. The Jewish inhabitants nearly starved to death as they refused to leave even one room of the homes and buildings they occupied. Valiant efforts were made both to supply the city with food and to take control of the city. The Israelis lost the battle for the city, although they won the larger war that enabled them to hold onto the land offered to them by the UN.

In 1967, when the Arab nations gathered to drive Israel into the sea, Israel begged Jordan not to engage in the conflict. Yet upon hearing stories of Arab victories over the Israelis, the Jordanians could not resist entering the war. The Israelis defeated the Arabs in the Six Day War. The Israelis took the opportunity to enter the city through the tiny St. Stephen's (or Lion's) Gate and seized control of the Temple Mount. Moshe Dayan, General of the Israeli army, ordered the troops off of the Mount immediately after taking control over it, the site of the Dome of the Rock. Although Israel maintains control of the Temple Mount, the military does not keep a presence there. Israel did however tear down the buildings blocking access to the Western Wall of the Ancient Temple (what many call the Wailing Wall) and built a pavilion so that all people could have access to the Wall for prayer. This action in June 1967 has set up the challenge to the world as to who should have authority over this three-thousand year old city, and more significantly who should oversee these holy sites.

The offenses each side has inflicted on the other are remembered and passed on from generation to generation. So today, both sides can recite atrocities perpetrated against them by their enemies for decades, even centuries ago, as if these events had occurred yesterday. Jerusalem, as it stands, is one reality. But the Jerusalem as it rages in the hearts of its citizens and peoples around the world, who all have some vested interest in the city, is very far removed from the silent stones that stand in that city.

The issue then is the heart of men and not the city itself. The Psalmist says *"the fool says in his heart there is no God"* (Psalm 14:1). Notice the Bible does not say that the fool says with his mouth that there is no God; he merely

. asserts such foolishness in his thoughts and meditations. He may proclaim loudly, *"Lord, Lord,"* but his actions demonstrate that his heart is far from the living God. *"These people draw near to Me with their mouth, and honor me with their lips. But their heart is far from Me and in vain they worship Me teaching as doctrines the commandments of men."* (Isaiah 29:13) Jerusalem is the highest evidence of the truth of God's Word that the issue is not one of zealous worship but a matter of the heart. The mouth asserts one thing but the reality is that the heart denies that God will someday judge the secrets of the heart. Each religion acts as if there were no ultimate judge of his beliefs and practices.

To assert that there is only one God is to proclaim that there is only one reality that is both physical and spiritual at one and the same time. Only one standard of justice and righteousness exists as God embodies righteousness and justice. All people will be judged by the same standard without exception. How can a religion claim to be monotheistic yet propose that there are varying standards of justice and righteousness?

The Dream

The dream is that the people of Jerusalem would, from their hearts, grieve over their own sin and offer forgiveness to those who have legitimately offended them. The Bible holds out such a dream in Zechariah 12:10. God is speaking and proclaims,

> *"And I will pour on the house of David and on the inhabitants of Jerusalem the Spirit of grace and supplication; then they will look on Me whom they pierced. Yes they will mourn for Him as one mourns for his only son and grieve for Him as one grieves for a firstborn."*

Not only the Jews but also all the inhabitants of Jerusalem will from their heart repent of their sins that nailed

17

Jesus to the cross. We cannot blame the Jews for the death of Messiah. Each of us needed our sin to be dealt with at the cross. Our guilt is what motivates us to grieve. We must stop accusing others while God is seeking to examine our conscience and lead us to repentance for our sins. The clear promise of God is that a day is coming when ALL the inhabitants of Jerusalem will mourn for THEIR sins, not someone else's. And the promise of God is in Zechariah 13:1, *"In that day a fountain shall be opened for the house of David and for the inhabitants of Jerusalem, for sin and uncleanness."* God will forgive the sins of all peoples, the Jew first but also the Arab, Armenian, and the professing Christian who never knew such genuine and sincere grief for sin nor such cleansing of heart and conscience. All will worship the Almighty together in unison - not in form but in joyfulness of heart that all the people in Jerusalem will have unity in worship to the Triune Savior. Former persecutors will seek forgiveness for their deeds of terror. Those who despised others of another nationality and religion will find joy as one holy nation set apart to serve as priests together praying for the conflicts of the world to cease. God's law will be honored and a government set up that will provide justice and mercy for all who have been oppressed. Those with wealth and abundance will share with those in need. There will be a love for the apostles' doctrine and teaching because now the people of Jerusalem will be lovers of truth and not merely lovers of religious forms that they learned by rote memory. Problems of the society will be solved because those called to govern will reason with Biblical reasoning from God's law. Rather than religion being destroyed as John Lennon "imagined," Biblical faith will be established and the joy of serving the living God will resound throughout the earth. This is not a dream any person could imagine for himself. Only God could give us such a dream of "all Israel" returning to their God and the Arabs likewise turning from their heart to worship the same God and for Jew and Arab to have a common view of justice and righteousness.

The Psalmist wrote of such a day and the Jewish people celebrated that vision as they ascended to Solomon's Temple. They sang,

"When the Lord brought back the captivity of Zion, we were like those who dream. Then our mouth was filled with laughter and our tongue with singing, then they said among the nations, the Lord has done great things for them. The Lord has done great things for us and we are glad" (Psalm 126:1-3).

The Jews are captive to their own rebellion against their covenant God who chose them and originally constituted them as a nation. We dream of their release from such a prison of confusion and unbelief into the liberty of worshipping the living God.

God Himself is committed to this dream. He Himself has set watchmen on the walls of Jerusalem who are never to hold their peace day or night. *"You who make mention of the Lord, do not keep silent, and give Him no rest till he establishes and till He makes Jerusalem a praise in all the earth"* (Isaiah 62:6-7). Imagine Jerusalem to be a praise before the nations rather than a cup of trembling in their hands, who are anxious and fearful that war will spread from Jerusalem and spill over into a worldwide conflict between the West and the Islamic states. God promises that *"Violence shall no longer be heard in the land neither devastation nor destruction within your borders; but you shall call your walls Salvation and your gates Praise"* (Isaiah 60:18).

Jerusalem will be the model for peace and harmony in the worship of the living God under the authority of God's Word. Palestinians and Jews, Armenians and Turks, Muslims and Christians from all over the world will unite as one holy nation under the good order of the Word of God and the law of God, grieving and repenting of their sin and rejoicing in the Almighty who laid our sin upon His Son and bruised Him for our iniquity. True worship will be the door of peace and joy for Jerusalem and for nations of the earth.

"For Zion's sake I will not hold my peace, and for Jerusalem's sake I will not rest until her righteousness goes forth as brightness and her salvation as a lamp that burns. The Gentiles will see your righteousness and all kings your glory" (Isaiah 62:1-2). So *"Arise, shine for your light has come! And the glory of the Lord has risen upon you. For behold the darkness covers the earth. And deep darkness the people; but the Lord will arise over you and His glory will be seen in you. The Gentiles shall come to your light and kings to the brightness of your rising."* (Isaiah 60:1-3)

This was the dream given to Peter at Pentecost when he proclaimed to thousands of Jewish people at the Temple, *"Therefore let all the house of Israel know assuredly that God has made this Jesus, whom you crucified both Lord and Christ"* (Acts 2:36). But all Israel did not "know" nor did they believe on that first day of Pentecost that Jesus was Lord and Messiah. "Only" three thousand believed. Merely a handful believed but not all the house of Israel. Was Peter disappointed at the response?

Let us *"pray for the peace of Jerusalem"* (Psalm 122:6). Such peace will come from the Holy Spirit moving and motivating "all the House of David" and "all the inhabitants of Jerusalem" to believe the promises God has offered to all in Jesus His Son. Someday all will know that God has made His Son both Lord and Messiah.

Will the whole house of Israel bow before that One who is the King of Kings and Lord of Lords? Can you dream the dream that all Israel will be saved? Along with the Jews returning to their God, can you dream that there will be a great turning of Islamic Arabs as well as Palestinians to genuine faith in Jesus as their Messiah who died on a Roman cross for sin? Can you believe that a genuine reformation and revival will move many peoples to repentance and genuine faith? When such a dream comes true, those of us who imagined such a dream will stand in awe that somehow we had dreamt this dream together with our God and with multitudes of others before us. These all died in faith never having seen this promised dream come to pass. When this dream comes to pass, we will be so filled with awe at what God has done that we will wonder if we are simply dreaming or if it is real. If you can consider even dreaming such a dream, *"Come now, and let us reason together"* (Isaiah 1:18).

Chapter 2

Why are the Jews a Priority?

Can you imagine a world without the Jews? Some would like to try, believing the world would be a better place without the Jewish people. Nevertheless, attempting to picture the world without the Jews would be like having a Bible without the Children of Israel or any of the history about the Jewish people. There have been those who would prefer a Reader's Digest version of the Bible that would be merely the systematic theology of the New Testament devoid of all these difficult and confusing stories in the Old Testament. The fact is that there is still an identifiable group of people called the Jews and the Bible is primarily about this people group. Have you ever asked yourself the question, "Why?"

The first eleven chapters of Genesis focus on those historical realities that affect us all: the creation, the fall of man into sin, the promise of God for the future, God's judgment on sin by the flood; yet also His preservation of the human race through Noah, the development of nations, and finally the Tower of Babel. In Genesis 12, God's strategy in dealing with the nations changes from dealing with all humanity to dealing with one man and one family – Abraham and his family. God's goal was to bless all the nations, yet the remainder of the Old Testament and the Gospels is about God's dealings with the Jews. Not until the book of Acts do we see the focus significantly expand to the nations of the earth.

The Living God makes clear His call upon Abraham's life, that *"in you all the families of the earth shall be blessed"* (Genesis 12:3). This promise was a multigenerational promise passed on to the son of Promise,

Isaac. Isaac was the Son that God had promised to Abraham and therefore he was the heir of this promise to be a blessing to the nations. Isaac was the only son, for he was the son of the covenant God made with Abraham to make him a blessing to the nations. By faith Jacob understood the significance of this covenant promise that was lost on Esau his brother. Esau consequently sold this blessing to meet his immediate needs, whereas Jacob was willing to pay any price to inherit the promise of God. Yet Jacob's rejoicing before God in prayer is *"I am not worthy of the least of all the mercies and of all the truth which You have shown Your servant . . ."* (Genesis 32:10). The Living God preserves His people through famine by means of Joseph. Four hundred years later, God filled out the covenant with Abraham by calling Israel out of Egypt and establishing the sons of Jacob as a nation by a definitive covenant with Moses.

Exodus 19-24 is the heart of that covenant with Moses that defines the relationship between God and His chosen people. As these chapters are read, we must always think of the relationship between God and His people that He delivered in the Exodus, delivered from by the Angel of Death in the Passover, and delivered through the Red Sea. God describes His action this way:

> *"You have seen what I did to the Egyptians, and how I bore you on eagle's wings and brought you to Myself. Now therefore, if you will indeed obey MY voice and keep my covenant, then you shall be a special treasure to Me above all people; for all the earth is Mine. 'And you shall be a kingdom of priests and a holy nation.'"* (Exodus 19:4-6)

The fifteenth century BC Middle Eastern Treaties between Great Kings and lesser kings who relied on the Great King for their protection followed a pattern clearly seen in Exodus 20. The pattern is:

1st   The Identification of the Great King
2nd   A History of the Relationship

3rd	Commandments: Requirements of the Relationship
4th	Sanctions: What Happens if the Commands are Honored and What Happens if They are Violated
5th	Covenant Continuity for the Future

The Ten Commandments passage in Exodus 20:1 begins with, *"I am the Lord your God who brought you out of the Land of Egypt, out of the house of bondage."* The Treaty form structuring a relationship between a King and His vassals is clearly seen: the Great King is identified, and their history of deliverance is affirmed. Therefore Exodus 20 is not merely the "Ten Commandments" but is clearly establishing a relationship between "I am, the Lord your God," the One who has graciously and sovereignly saved you in time and history from the house of bondage; therefore keep these commands if you desire to be blessed in this relationship. The history of the relationship is followed by the requirements of the commandments. Exodus 20 clearly falls into the category of the fifteenth century BC Middle Eastern Treaties of Great Kings discovered by archaeologists and identified by Meridith Kline and others.

The book of Deuteronomy is the second repetition of this covenant treaty to preserve the relationship for future generations, as Moses was about to die and a successor was needed.

Deuteronomy 1:1- 6 identifies the sovereign king, *"the Lord our God."* Deuteronomy 1:7-3:29 updates the history since the last covenant ceremony at Sinai. Deuteronomy 4:1-26:19 restates the law and expands on the meaning of the commandments and then in Deuteronomy 27-30, the Covenant God expands on the sanctions, the curse and the blessings that would result from either disobedience or obedience to this covenant. This section of the Bible describes the history of the Jews for the past 2500 years. These words are more up to date than the morning news. This covenant is a fulfillment of the Promise to Abraham as God says:

"that you may enter into covenant with the Lord your God and into His oath, which the Lord makes with you today, that He may establish you as a people for Himself, and that He may be God to you, just as He has spoken to you, and just as He has sworn to your fathers, to Abraham, Isaac and Jacob." (Deuteronomy 29:12-13)

As with all legal documents, witnesses are required. Both heaven and earth are the witnesses because no other person, other than God, will endure forever. Jesus calls upon these witnesses in Matthew 5:18, asserting that until heaven and earth pass away, not one jot nor one tittle of the law will fail.

God's Covenant to All Future Generations of Israelites

Yet this covenant is not only made with the people who entered the Promised land under Joshua in 1410 B.C., but God asserts, *"I make this covenant, not with you alone..."*, but also with those of future generations, for this revealed covenant is for *"our children forever"* (Deuteronomy 29:14, 29). Failure to keep the covenant and honor the Great King who is Creator and Lord over all the earth will result in all nations asking, *"Why has the Lord done so to this land? What does the heat of this great anger mean?"* (Deuteronomy 29:24) The answer is,

"Because they have forsaken the covenant of the Lord God of their fathers which He made with them when He brought them out of the land of Egypt...Then the anger of the Lord was aroused against this land, to bring on it every curse that was written in this book, And the Lord uprooted them from their land in anger, in wrath and in much indignation, and cast them into another land as it is this day." (Deuteronomy 29:25-28)

As recipients of the promise given to Abraham, Israel is to be a blessing to the nations. Israel is a testimony to the nations either in their cursing or in their blessing. The history of Israel is history. No other nation captures God's dealings with all mankind as does the history of the Jewish people. Scripture records various examples of God's miraculous provision by helping Israel. For example, the parting of the Jordan River when Israel entered Canaan so that *"all the peoples of the earth may know the hand of the Lord, that it is mighty, that you may fear the Lord your God forever"* (Joshua 4:24). When David challenged Goliath, he proclaimed, *"this day the Lord will deliver you into my hand and I will strike you and take your head from you ... that all the earth may know that there is a God in Israel"* (1 Samuel 17:46).

Psalm 67 clearly sings of God's purpose for His people: *"God be merciful to us and bless us and cause your face to shine on us, that your way may be known on earth, your salvation among all the nations."* The blessings God showers upon Israel are a testimony to all the nations on earth. Israel is God's "pilot project" before all the other nations. If Israel obeys the truth and worships the living God then the nations of the world will follow their testimony. If Israel fails it will mean trouble to the nations. Yet the Lord promises in Deuteronomy 30:5-6:

> *"then the Lord your God will bring you to the land which your fathers possessed, and you shall possess it. He will prosper you and multiply you more than your fathers. And the Lord your God will circumcise your heart and the hearts of your descendants, to love the Lord the Lord your God with all your heart, with all your soul, that you may live."*

For this reason, the Apostle Paul asserts in Romans 1:16, *"I am not ashamed of the Gospel of Christ for it is the power of God unto salvation for everyone who believes to the Jew first, and also to the Gentile."* The Jews are an identifiable group of people. What unifies Jewish people is their keeping of the holy days such as Passover, Yom Kippur and Succoth. Jewish people are united as they light the candles, put on the prayer shawl and use their Passover plates. Regardless of whether one is Orthodox, Conservative or Reformed, these rituals bind the people together. Hebrew is a living language to vast numbers of Jews who make great efforts to learn this language, even to the far corners of the earth. The modern state of Israel gives meaning and identity to the Jews. They have a stake in the success of Israel because it is viewed as a refuge to them. They believe that if Jews are not safe in Israel they are not safe anywhere on the earth. Is it an accident that in spite of having intermarried with many other nationalities, the Jews are still an identifiable group of people?

Ironically, what threatens Jewish identity is faith in Jesus. To the mind of the majority of Jews, belief in Jesus disqualifies them from being Jewish. Is the gospel of Jesus Christ powerful enough to transform Jewish people from those who categorically reject Jesus as Savior to those reconciled with the God of their fathers, Abraham, Isaac and Jacob? Paul asserts that the gospel is powerful enough. *"For I am not ashamed of the gospel of Christ, for it is the power of God to salvation for everyone who believes, for the Jew first and also for the Greek"* (Romans 1:16).

The evangelization of the Jewish people must be made a priority in world missions. As John Calvin writes in his commentary on Zechariah 12:10:

> "That the Jews previously so hardened in their evils, as not to flee to God for help, would become at length suppliants, because the Spirit would inwardly so touch their hearts as to lead them to deplore their state before God and thus to express their complaints to Him."(p. 362)

> Again, Calvin writes, "Now as Zechariah declares that the Jews would at length look to God, it follows, that the spirit of repentance and the light of faith are

27

promised to them so that they might know God as the author of their salvation and feel so assured that they are saved as in the future to devote themselves entirely to Him: they shall then look to me whom they pierced. Here also the Prophet indirectly reproves the Jews for their great obstinacy, for God had restored them....for their piercing is to be taken metaphorically for continual provocation as though he has said that the Jews in their perverseness were prepared for war, that they goaded and pierced God by their wickedness or by the weapons of their rebellion...He says now that such a change would be wrought by God that they would become quite different, for they would learn to look to him whom they had previously pierced." (p. 363)

Calvin comments on the promise in Zechariah 13:1

"...that though the Jews had in various ways defiled themselves, so that they were become filthy before God, and their uncleanness was abominable, yet a fountain would be prepared for them, by which they might cleanse themselves so as to come before God pure and clean."

God had

"even provided for them a cleansing by the blood of His only-begotten Son, so that no filth might prevent them to call on Him boldly and in confidence; for instead of legal rites there would be the reality, as their hearts would be sprinkled by the Spirit, so that they would be purified by faith, and would thus cast away all their filth." (p. 377)

The issue is not only one of rejecting Jesus as Messiah but also the rejection of the Covenant Lord who constituted Israel as a nation 3500 years ago and has called Israel to be the a light to the nations. If this rebellion of the Jews to their national calling were faced, then the salvation offered in the same Messiah would have meaning to them.

Is it possible that the Palestinian terrorist bombers are God's means of calling Israel to repentance as they mourn for their dead? Will they ever question themselves as to why God has called them to such suffering? When will they mourn for their sin? "Blessed are those who mourn for they shall be comforted," assures Jesus in Matthew 5:4. Is the ultimate solution to conflict between the Palestinians and Israel a "peace treaty" forced upon the two peoples by outside governments? On June 6, 2003, Prime Minister Ariel Sharon of Israel and Prime Minister Mahmoud Abbas of the Palestinian Authority met with President Bush of the United States in Aqaba, Jordan to develop the "Roadmap for Peace" for Israel and the Palestinians. Within seven days three terrorist attacks killed twenty-three Israelis. Both sides talk of peace but the most a government can hope for is a cessation of hostilities. Peace must come from changed hearts and attitudes. No government can impose genuine peace. Are these attacks outside of the sovereign control of the Almighty God? Or is the covenant God of Abraham, Moses, and David calling His chosen people to repentance? A change is needed from the inside out rather than an imposed "peace plan" that requires armies to enforce from the outside in. Is the Living God able to bring peace to the Jews?

For centuries, the Jewish people themselves misunderstood their privileged place in God's plan for history by gloating over their being the chosen people. They confidently trusted that they were nearer to God simply by being Jewish. During the time of Jesus, Jews despised the Gentiles, even calling them "dogs." Jewish men thanked God that he did not create them as Gentiles. Such ethnic pride still is a barrier to genuine repentance.

For 2500 years Jewish people, as a race of people, have despised their own covenant role in being a "light to the nations". Will the Jewish people take responsibility for their sins against their Covenant King and Lord? When the Jews turn to their God, the God of Abraham, Isaac and Jacob, then the joyful invitation to the nations will be spoken:

> *"Hear the Word of the Lord O nations and declare it to the isles afar off, and say 'He who scattered Israel will gather him . . . therefore they shall come and sing in the height of Zion, streaming to the goodness of the Lord . . ."* (Jeremiah 31:10-12)

God has made the Jews of utmost significance and to diminish their place in history is to resist the Creator God of the Bible. The Jewish people are significant for their testimony and witness to the rest of the world. Will they take their leadership role before the nations? Historically, as Paul Johnson testifies in <u>A History of the Jews</u>, "They always knew that Jewish society was appointed as a pilot project for the entire human race. That Jewish dilemmas, dramas and catastrophes should be exemplary, larger than life, would seem only natural to them" (p. 587). Is it possible the Jews could provide an example of grief for sin and of faith in that One who provides a cleansing fountain for all unrighteousness?

Chapter 3

The Gentile Church's Relationship to the Jews

The Apostle Paul's strategy for ministering the gospel to his brethren in Israel was to evangelize the Gentiles so that a Gentile church that delighted in the Messiah would create a jealousy amongst the Jews to believe in their own Messiah. *"I say then, have they stumbled that they should fall? Certainly not! But through their fall, to provoke them to jealousy, salvation has come to the Gentiles"* (Romans 11:11). Paul definitely took the long multigenerational view with regard to his ministry. Two thousand years after Paul's ministry, the vision of a Gentile church creating jealousy amongst the Jews motivating them to faith in Christ has not happened.

In fact, rather than provoking the Jews to jealousy, the Gentile church simply provoked the Jews. Instead of being a blessing to the Jews, the Gentile church cursed the Jews. Paul celebrated in Ephesians 2:19 that the Gentiles who had been strangers to the covenant of promise now *"were no longer strangers and foreigners, but fellow citizens with the saints and members of the household of God . . ."* Throughout the first century, Gentiles were the minority among the community of faith celebrating Jesus as Messiah. There grew together two communities of faith: those who were Nazarenes, Jews who believed in Jesus and lived an 'observant' lifestyle by keeping kosher (Acts 24:5), and those who were Christians, a mixed group of Jews and Gentiles who were not committed to circumcision or a law-observant lifestyle. *"The disciples were first called Christians at Antioch"* (Acts 11:26). The Christians were a mixed group of Gentiles and Hellenistic Jews in contrast to the much more observant Jerusalem Jews.

Although the Jewish believers graciously received Gentile believers into their midst and provided Biblical counsel and direction for the young church, in time, by the second century, Gentile believers outnumbered Jewish believers. In addition, there was great prejudice and hatred for all that was Jewish. The destruction of Jerusalem in 70 AD demonstrated the great hatred Romans had for the Jews. Roman emperors attempted to execute any Jew who claimed to descend from King David. The emperor Hadrian rebuilt the city of Jerusalem along Roman lines so that there would be no memory of Jewish presence there. Whereas during the Temple period Jerusalem was a temple with a small city around it, now Jerusalem was a city with many smaller temples dedicated to pagan deities rather than the God of Israel.

The early Christians called the Jews to repentance in response to their hard-heartedness to their God and their Messiah. Paul wrote in 1 Thessalonians 2:14-16:

> *"For you brethren, became imitators of the churches of God which are in Judea in Christ Jesus. For you also suffered the same things from your own country men, just as they did from the Jews, who killed both the Lord Jesus and their own prophets, and have persecuted us; and they do not please God and are contrary to all men, forbidding us to speak to the Gentiles that they may be saved, so as always to fill up the measure of their sins; but wrath has come upon them to the uttermost."*

Paul does not cover up the Jews' rebellion against the Lord, yet his heart's desire was for the salvation of his countrymen (Romans 9:1-3). He is not callous toward their spiritual condition. Paul is not bitter towards the Jews who beat him five times with 39 lashes of the whip. His seemingly harsh evaluation is to call the Jews to repentance, not to write them off as hopeless.

Stephen likewise preached to his countrymen in Acts 7. He recounts God's dealings with the Jewish people from Abraham through Moses and David. He then asks the question of the Jewish leadership:

"Which of the prophets did your fathers not persecute? And they killed those who foretold the coming Just One of who you have become betrayers and murderers who have received the law by the direction of angels and have not kept it." (Acts 7: 52-53)

Stephens's goal of preaching the sermon was to call the Jews to repentance. Stephen demonstrated the heart of the prophet whose words tore God's people apart but yet also spoke the word to comfort their faithless hearts. Later Gentile preachers changed the focus from a prophetic call to repentance to a prejudicial statement of despair and rejection of Jewish people because of their ethnic character.

"We see this clearly in Justin Martyr:

If you (Jews) will confess the truth, you yourselves cannot deny that we (Gentiles) are more faithful than you in relation to God. For we, having been called of God by means of the mystery of the cross, which is so despised and full of shame; and (suffering) punishments even unto death for our confession and obedience and piety. . . we, I say, endure all things lest we should deny Christ even in word. But you were redeemed from Egypt with a high arm and a visitation of great glory (there follows an extensive enumeration of all the wonders worked by God for the benefit of Israel during the desert wandering). In spite of all this you made a calf, and eagerly committed fornication with the daughters of the aliens, and committed idolatry, and did so again afterwards when the land had been entrusted to you with such great power . . . You are convicted by the prophets, even after Moses' warnings, of having, in

33

addition to all this, dared so much against Christ, and still do dare. (Dialogue with Trypho 131.2-133.1)

As can be seen from this excerpt, Justin has full biblical support for everything he says about the Jewish nation. And yet the distance from the Old Testament and from Stephen's speech is enormous. For in Justin the enumeration of Israel's sins is no longer meant to be a call to repentance and return to God. In Justin it has become something quite different: Justin takes the biblical record of Israel's sins to mean that the Jews have a natural inclination toward disbelief and sin, while claiming that the Gentiles have a natural inclination toward belief and obedience. The ruthless Jewish self-criticism contained in several passages in the Old Testament – unparalleled in the ancient world and one of the finest fruits of Mosaic and prophetic teaching – is misused by Justin as if it were some kind of ethnological description of the peculiarities of the Jewish people."[1]

By the early third century, the apologist Origen claimed that all of the promises to Israel were now transferred to the Church of Christ. The Gentile church, instead of standing in solidarity with the Jewish church, broke away from the Jewish church and exploited passages where the sins of the Jews had been enumerated for the purpose of calling Jews to repentance and instead used these against the Jews to write them off as hopeless. When Constantine professed Christianity and the Edict of Milan granted toleration to Christians in 313 AD, the church became increasingly disconnected from its Jewish roots. Constantine sent his mother to Israel to identify the sites that were connected to the life of Jesus and built churches over those sites so that they were no longer identifiable as Jewish sites but became "Christian" sites. The country became "the Holy Land" and ceased being Jewish. Likewise, those Jews who did profess faith in Jesus as their Messiah were required to renounce all Jewish practices.

"I renounce all customs, rites, legalisms, unleavened breads and sacrifices of lambs of the Hebrews, and all the other feasts of the Hebrews, sacrifices, prayers, aspersions, purifications, sanctifications and propitiations, and fasts, and new moons, and Sabbaths, and superstitions, and hymns and chants and observances and synagogues, and the food and drink of the Hebrews; in one word, I renounce absolutely everything Jewish, every law, rite and custom. . . .and if afterwards I shall wish to deny and return to Jewish superstition, or shall be found eating with Jews, or feasting with them, or secretly conversing and condemning the Christian religion instead of openly confuting them and condemning their vain faith, then let the trembling of Cain and leprosy of Gehazi cleave to me, as well as the legal punishments to which I acknowledge myself liable. And may I be anathema in the world to come, and may my soul be set down with Satan and the devils."[2]

Jewish life was completely forbidden by the Roman church. Professing Jewish believers could not keep any of their Jewish cultural practices. As Eusebius, the first church historian, records the growth of the church in the year 315 A.D., he totally ignores the existence of this Nazarene church. To the Roman Catholic church, the Nazarene church never did exist. But such histories affect us as well because we know so little about the first Nazarene believers, and we act as if all of the early Christians were Gentiles. In fact, just the opposite is true; nearly all the early Christians were Jews.

During this same period, mainstream Jews were busy redefining Judaism as well. As a result, after the destruction of the Temple in 70 AD, the Jews needed to re-identify themselves because the center of their faith, the Temple, was now gone. Who were they as Jews? Increasingly because of the hatred and persecution by the Christian church, mainstream Jews identified their faith by their unbelief in Jesus as Messiah. This conflict between church and synagogue grew so that by the 11th century, hatred could easily be stirred against Jews.

"As the influence of the clergy widened and the Church orders gained in power, local persecutions became common. An envenomed sermon by an ignorant fanatic often impelled the simple folks of a community to burn down synagogues and homes and to lay violent hands on the Jews. It became an annual custom in Beziers, in the week between Palm Sunday and Easter Monday, when the priests described the sufferings of Jesus, to pelt the Jews with mud and stones whenever they appeared. In Toulouse, the Count in the city had the right to slap the face of the Jewish leader on Good Friday."[3]

Such persecution resulted in the Jews being expelled from France in 1394 and from Spain in 1492. The Inquisition in Spain resulted in the execution of 30,000 to 50,000 Jews. In the 16th century, Martin Luther at first had hopes of the Jews converting in great numbers to become believers in Christ. When they did not, he became disillusioned. In his disillusionment he proclaimed that the remedy for the Jews' unbelief was:

"'First, their synagogues should be set on fire, and whatever is left should be buried in dirt so that no one may ever be able to see a stone or cinder of it. 'Jewish prayer-books should be destroyed and rabbis forbidden to preach. Then the Jewish people should be dealt with, their homes 'smashed and destroyed' and their inmates 'put under one roof or in a stable like gypsies, to teach them they are not master in our land.' Jews should be banned from the roads and markets, their property seized and then these 'poisonous envenomed worms' should be drafted into forced labor and made to earn their bread 'by the sweat of their noses.'"[4]

This heritage of hatred for the Jews that endured for over 500 years was passed on, climaxing in the Holocaust. Hitler did not create such hatred but simply built on the foundation of prejudice entrenched within the church as well as European society; he capitalized on an existing mindset.

"The missionaries of Christianity had said in effect: You have no right to live among us as Jews. The secular rulers who followed had proclaimed: You have no right to live among us. The German Nazis at last decreed: You have no right to live." [5]

The Jews, in response to such Christian persecution, have determined that as Jews you can believe almost anything, but you cannot believe in Jesus. It is assumed universally by Jews that once you believe in Jesus as Messiah then you can no longer be a Jew. So Jewish people feel easily threatened by any attempt to cvangclizc them as an attempt to destroy their Jewishness, or worse yet, a type of genocide.

In 1958 the Israeli cabinet with the counsel of Jewish communities both inside and outside of Israel, decided that even if a Jewish person forsakes the Jewish religion, that person is still a Jew so long as he or she does not accept another religion.

"What religion did they have in mind? Not Zen Buddhism. Not Hare Krishna. Not Humanism. No, the only religion they objected to was Christianity."[6] "It is the rejection of Jesus as Christ that binds American Jews together. It is by the rejection of the Messiahship of Jesus that we proclaim to the world that we are still Jews."[7] So it is the Christian Church that has helped define the Jews as to their identity over the centuries. As Paul says, *"concerning the gospel they are enemies for your sake."* (Romans 11:28) **There is truly a great chasm between church and synagogue initiated by the church and deepened by Jewish leadership.**

Instead of provoking the Jews to jealousy so that they would desire to receive Jesus as their Messiah, the opposite has occurred. Gentiles defined a Jew who believes in Jesus as Messiah as one who is no longer a Jew. The Jewish leadership has agreed and declared that any Jew who professes to believe in Jesus is no longer Jewish. Christian missionaries are then considered threats not only to the religion of the Jewish people but also to Jewish cultural and national identity.

Is the gospel powerful enough to break through these centuries-old barriers of bitterness and offense by the Gentile church toward the Jews? Paul asserted, *"I am not ashamed of the gospel of Christ for it is the power of God unto salvation to everyone who believes, to the Jew first and also to the Gentile"* (Romans 1:16).

Chapter 4

The Heritage

Jewish people for centuries have wondered why they cannot be accepted just as other people. Why are Jews separated out from everyone else and then held up to derision? This is a perplexity both to Jews and those who do discriminate against them. Medieval society, as it came increasingly under the control and influence of the Roman Catholic Church, unified all of society around their faith. The Jews were not a part of that society and therefore were increasingly excluded. The Jews were pushed into ghettoes where they developed an alternative society. They could not be a part of the trade unions, societies, or even receive legal protections by the feudal courts. Jews learned to deal in paper assets, as their wealth was continually stolen and paper assets made it more difficult for theft. The Jews developed their own alternative news system over the centuries. Paper wealth creation is largely the contribution of the Jews. Likewise, Reuters and other news agencies were of Jewish origin.

Ghettoes surrounded by large walls were not only required by townspeople in medieval Europe but they were also the choice of the Jews themselves. They could be more secure in ghettoes. The ghetto allowed them to maintain their peculiar lifestyle without interference from the Gentile world. Tradition could guide their lives rather than the ever-changing conventions of Gentile society. If segregation, as the church claimed, safeguarded Christians from evil Jewish contacts, likewise it equally protected Jews from secularity. The orthodox communities that exist in Brooklyn and Israel today are remnants of these Jewish communities.

The Reformation changed the fate of the Jews as the unified society that the Roman Catholic Church had created was broken apart. Roman Catholic bishops accused the Jews of encouraging the Reformers and blaming the Jews for motivating the Reformers. But the Reformers had rediscovered the Old Testament which was for all intents and purposes lost for centuries through questionable Bible interpretation and displaced by the fanciful interpretation of the allegorical method. The Reformed discovery of the doctrine of justification by faith also renewed interest in the law of God. A super-pious practice of repentance had moved professing Christians further and further away from what it meant to worship and obey God. The Reformers understood justification through the Son of God, who fulfilled the requirements of God's law on behalf of sinners, whereby Christ's righteousness is imputed to the believer. Not only had Jesus died to pay the penalty for sin, but He rose again so that the believer may be credited with the righteousness of Christ, rather than having to become righteous in order to be accepted by God. Repentance was to turn from disobedience to God's law and embrace Christ, enabling one to live a life of obedience. God's law then became the foundation for government, learning, science and all of life. Hence, all of the society was reformed by the Bible. God's law was King, and even the earthly king had to submit to the law of God.

The Reformation brought renewed interest in Hebrew studies and the Old Testament. Because of the interest of Reformation pastors and theologians, Protestant support grew for the Jews. Cromwell's England was the first real flowering of Jewish support as many Jews moved to England in the mid-seventeenth century. Because at that time only English law was based on the Bible, Jews were given protections not available in any other country. Today, in more than half the world, Jews speak English because they found stability and protection in British Commonwealth countries, and later the U.S.A.

Principles of interpreting the Bible changed from the spiritual guesswork of the allegorical method of interpretation that allowed for almost any kind of fanciful interpretation of the Scripture to the historical-grammatical method. The allegorical method of Bible interpretation did not require any knowledge of the historical setting of the Scriptures. The Reformers committed themselves to understanding the Biblical text in its original historical context. The Reformation hope of a revival among Jews to faith in Jesus became united with the hope for a homeland for the Jewish people. In the nineteenth century as Jews returned, so did Christians who developed the science of archaeology to assist in Biblical interpretation. With this interest in the historical roots of the Bible, gradually Christians developed a hope for a national homeland for the Jews. In the Puritan attempt to purify the Anglican Church and their country, preachers identified strongly with the efforts of the Old Testament children of Israel. The pilgrims in New England from 1620 onward saw their entire mission as a new Israel developing a new "city upon the hill" as a witness to the nations.

What drove the dream was the view that all Israel would be saved. As the Reformed pastor and commentator Robert Haldane wrote on Romans 11:23:

> "The Apostle having from the beginning of the 17th verse pressed upon the believing Gentiles the necessity of humility, now reverts to the subject of the future conversion of the Jews. In order to furnish a new proof of this great event, he introduces a fourth argument of the power of God. 'God is able to graft them in again'. When branches are severed from a tree, they wither and cannot be replaced. Paul therefore here refers to the power of God." What is there that God cannot do? "He is able to make the dry bones live and to restore the severed branches of the Jewish nation. Some argue that because the grafting of the Jews into the olive tree here spoken of is

conditional, it is not promised." Paul is demonstrating the power of God at least holds out the possibility of the Jews national conversion to faith in Jesus as their Messiah. Only unbelief will keep them from being saved. 'If that sin were subdued, they would be received. God is able to graft them in if they believe and He is able to give them faith."[1]

Such faith in the dream of a national conversion of the Jews energized the establishment of societies in the 19th century to evangelize the Jews. Theodore Herzl, founder of Zionism, found his first supporters in London because of centuries of Biblical teaching and writings that motivated the British to pray for the "peace of Jerusalem."

The Palestine Exploration society, made up entirely of Christians, published proposals for settlement of the Holy Land long before any Jews seriously were considering this thought.[2] The Historical method of Bible interpretation motivated archaeologists to go to Palestine for research. The Ottoman Turks, who ruled Palestine, had no interest in improving the land which they had abused and destroyed as documented in Mark Twain's popular book Innocents Abroad. Dreams of both the conversion of the Jews and further archaeological finds surrounded the hopes of Jews having a national homeland in Palestine.

Nations by the nineteenth century were built upon law and not upon race or the Divine right of Kings. People were viewed as bearing responsibility for their nation rather than as mere pawns in the hands of a monarch. Every community, city or nation had benefited from the presence of the Jews as the prophet Jeremiah had commanded the Jewish people in exile,

> "Build houses and dwell in them, plant gardens and eat the fruit. Take wives and beget sons and daughters; and take wives for your sons and give daughters to husbands so that they hear sons and daughters—that you may be increased and not

42

diminished. And seek the peace of the city where I have caused you to be captive and pray to the Lord for it, for in its peace you will have peace." (Jeremiah 29:5-7)

The amazing reality is that the Jews as a people were so patiently submissive to whatever was asked of them, even resigning themselves to oppression. They often believed whatever harsh treatment they received was deserved. Many believed that that they were being punished for their sins and when God considered them to have suffered enough and had fulfilled their redemption then God would send the Messiah. Rather than repent they would rather sacrifice themselves. God says that obedience is better than sacrifice (1 Samuel 15:2-23) and that submitting to God's righteousness and trusting that God has provided righteousness for His people in Christ is better than attempting to establish one's own righteousness.

The message proclaimed by the Reformers changed history. On the whole, 16th through 19th century Reformers believed that Christ's kingdom would come when "we pray that the kingdom of sin and Satan may be destroyed, the gospel propagated throughout the world, the Jews called, the fullness of the Gentiles brought in..." (Westminster Larger Catechism Question and Answer 191). This is what the Lord's Prayer teaches us to pray in the petition, *"Thy Kingdom come."*

Puritans such as Richard Sibbes taught that "the faithful Jews rejoiced to think of the calling of the Gentiles and why should not we joy to think of the calling of the Jews." The 17th century Puritan William Perkins taught:

"The Lord saith, 'All nations shall be blessed in Abraham.' Hence I gather that the nation of the Jews shall be called, and converted to the participation of this blessing: when and how, God knows; but that it shall be done before the end of the world we know."

And Elnathan Parr in the 17th century stated:

> "The casting off of the Jews, was our calling; but the calling of the Jews shall not be our casting off, but our greater enriching in grace, and that two ways: First, in regard of the company of believers, when the thousands of Israel shall come in, which shall doubtless cause many Gentiles which now lie in ignorance, error and doubt, to receive the gospel and join with . . . Secondly, in respect of the graces, which shall then in more abundance be rained down upon the Church."

John Calvin, although tending to identify Israel with the elect, still saw a place for ethnic Israel:

> "I extend the word *Israel* to all the people of God, according to this meaning, - When the Gentiles shall come in, the Jews also shall return from their defection to the obedience of faith; and thus shall be completed the salvation of the whole Israel of God, which must be gathered from both; and yet in such a way that the Jews shall obtain the first place, being as it were the first born in God's family."

The Jews have a pre-eminence as a nation whom God had preferred to all nations.[3] The Reformation resulted in different Protestant groups such as the Huguenots suffering under persecution and enabling them to identify with the Jews in their persecution. For example, the Scottish Covenanters instructed their praying societies to first of all pray "that the off cast Israel . . . would never be forgotten . . . that the promised day of their ingrafting again by faith be hastened." This doctrine of the Lord's saving the Jewish people grew out of the Reformation understanding of the Bible. Jonathan Edwards certainly prophesied the national conversion of the Jews when he wrote:

> "Jewish infidelity shall be overthrown . . . the Jews in all their dispersions shall cast away their old

infidelity, and shall have their hearts wonderfully changed, and abhor themselves for their past unbelief and obstinacy. They shall flow together to the blessed Jesus, penitently, humbly, and joyfully owning him as their glorious King and only Savior, and shall with all their hearts, as one heart and voice, declare his praises unto other nations. . . Nothing is more certainly foretold than this national conversion of the Jews in Romans 11."

Matthew Henry writes:

"Now two things he exhorts the Gentiles to, with reference to the rejected Jews: - To have a respect for the Jews, notwithstanding, and to desire their conversion. This is intimated in the prospect he gives them of the advantage that would accure to the church by their conversion, Romans 11:12, 15. It would be as life from the dead; and therefore they must not insult or triumph over those poor Jews, but rather pity them, and desire their welfare, and long for the receiving of them in again.

Another thing that qualifies this doctrine of the Jews' rejection is that, though for the present they are cast off, yet the rejection is not final; but, when the fullness of time is come, they will be taken in again. They are not cast off for ever, but mercy is remembered in the midst of wrath."

This hope motivated the 19th century missionaries such as Andrew Bonar and Robert Murray McCheyne to travel all over Europe and the Middle East in 1849 to discover how many Jews there were and what it would take to evangelize them. This was the beginning of modern Jewish evangelism and it grew out of the conviction that the conversion of the Jews would result in a great blessing of witnesses to all the Gentile nations as well.

Charles Hodge, the great Reformed theologian of the 19th century and professor at Princeton Seminary, wrote in his commentaries on Romans 11:26:

> "'And so all Israel shall be saved, as it is written.' Israel, here, from the context, must mean the Jewish people, and all Israel, the whole nation. The Jews, as a people, are now rejected; as a people, they are to be restored. As their rejection, although national, did not include the rejection of every individual; so their restoration, although in like manner national, need not be assumed to include the salvation of every individual Jew. All Israel is not therefore to be here understood to mean, all the true people of God, as Augustine, Calvin, and many others explain it; nor all the elect Jews, i.e., all that part of the nation which constitute 'the remnant according to the election of grace;' but the whole nation, as a nation."

And again Charles Hodge says on the text of Romans 11:15:

> "this event has been facilitated, as remarked above, by the Jews; what will the restoration of the Jews then be, but life from the dead? That is, it will be a most glorious event; as though a new world had risen, not only glorious in itself, but in the highest degree beneficial to the Gentiles."

In the 20th century, John Murray, the professor at Westminster Theological Seminary, comments on Romans 11:

> "Israel are both 'enemies' and 'beloved' at the same time, enemies as regards the gospel, beloved as regards the election . . . 'Beloved' thus means that God has not suspended or rescinded his relation to Israel as his chosen people in terms of the covenants made with their fathers. Unfaithful as Israel has been and broken off for that reason, yet God still sustains his peculiar relation of love to them, a relation that

46

will be demonstrated and vindicated in the restoration."

These are only a sampling of the texts that demonstrate how this doctrine has deeply imbedded the Church. In the late 19th century, another view known as Dispensationalism viewed God as having two ways of salvation, one for the Jews through the Mosaic Law and another through the gospel in the "Church age". This theological view believed that when the Jewish people rejected Christ, then the "mystery age" of the Gentile Church began. When God completed His work with the Church then the Church would be secretly raptured and God would return to fulfill His promises to the Jews. As a consequence, a kind of anti-Semitism seeped anew into the Church. As a result of this theological view, some saw the way of salvation for the Jews as separate from the way of salvation to the Gentiles. Jewish evangelism lost its priority during this age to await the time after the Rapture. Others considered evangelizing the Jews as too offensive to even attempt. Therefore, the Reformers' hopes became distorted into support for the State of Israel whether they acted justly or unjustly. The amillenial view saw the Jews as having had their opportunity to receive Jesus as their Messiah, and having largely rejected Christ as Savior, they are to get in line with other nations to receive the gospel.

Yet the Apostle Paul asserts that the gospel is powerful for the Jews. They need the Savior today as do all peoples. We must once again reignite the restoration hope of ministry of the gospel to the Jews as a priority. We must dream of the mass conversion of Israel and pray for the peace of Jerusalem. What could be more anti-Semitic than to fail to proclaim the gospel to the Jewish people who proclaimed the truth of the gospel to Gentiles so long ago?

Chapter 5

A Realistic Dream

Is the dream that large numbers of Jewish people will come to faith in Jesus as Messiah a meaningful hope, even though there has always been a faithful remnant of Jews who are believers? As Paul proclaimed in Romans 11:5, *"Even so at this present time there is a remnant according to the election of grace."* All the early Christians were Jewish although some Jews didn't believe Gentiles could become believers in Jesus while others thought they had to first become Jewish proselytes in order to become believers in Jesus. (Acts 15:22-29) Besides being a history of the early church, the whole purpose of the book of Acts was to give Jewish believers the hope that Gentiles could also know God through Jesus the Messiah. It took a vision from God to get Peter to share the gospel with a Gentile in Acts 10. The gospel quickly spread among those Gentiles who were already open to the teaching of the Jews, but there were distinctions from the beginning between the Gentile believers who were called Christians, and the other Jewish believers, including Paul, who were known as Nazarenes. Both Gentile and Jewish believers were viewed as a Jewish sect by the Jewish community and by the Roman government (Acts 24:5), and so they were one sect with two distinct streams under the one religion of Judaism. As a reorganized religion in the Roman Empire, Christians were given protections they otherwise would not have had.

The history of Jewish believers is difficult to trace because it is so tied together with the Jewish people as a whole. In the year 68 AD and prior to the Roman army circling Jerusalem, the believers in Jesus heeding His words in Luke 21:20-24, fled the city and gathered in Pella across the Jordan River (Eusebius, Book 3, section 5). The Jews referred to those who fled Jerusalem as the "Meshumadim," or traitors, a term that is still used today of Hebrew Christians by the Orthodox Jewish leaders. This was the first time that there was a distinction made between the Nazarene Jews and their Gentile/Jewish brothers. After the destruction of Jerusalem, Jewish Christians or Nazarenes remained a distinct community but they lived as Jews in general reconciliation with the Jewish community until 132-135 AD. In these three years a Jewish revolt against Rome broke out again, this time under the leadership of Bar Kochba. The Jewish Christians fought together with their Jewish brothers side by side against Rome until Rabbi Akiba proclaimed Bar Kochba the Messiah. The Nazarene believers found this proclamation untenable so they could no longer support the revolt and refused to fight because Jesus of Nazareth was their Messiah, not Bar Kochba. At this point a complete break took place between the Nazarene Jewish believers and the Jews who pronounced this curse on them: "Let there be no hope for the apostates and let all the sectarians perish in a moment." The Jewish believers were thrown out of the Jewish communities. The growing separation between the Church and synagogue left the Nazarenes despised by both the Jews and the Gentile Christians.

Now one would have thought that the Gentile believers would welcome their Jewish brothers, but in fact Gentiles scorned them. This scorn deepened as a result of the rise to power of Constantine who proclaimed Christianity as the state religion and called for the council of Nicea in 325 AD. Freedom for the persecuted Christians did not result in sympathy and love for the Jews, but instead a systematic persecution of Jews by Roman Christians against the Nazarene believers began that lasted for the next 1200 years. Constantine sent his mother to Jerusalem and Palestine to "discover" the places holy in the life of Jesus, many of these places had become sites of Nazarene churches such as Peter's house in Capernaum. The Nazarene believers were driven from their churches and these sites were taken over by the Byzantine government. Initially these sites became a part of Gentile Christian service and later they became sites for pilgrims to come and worship. After 300 years as centers of worship, these sites attained the status of "holy." The Nazarene believers were despised as a group and moved out of their places of worship as Byzantine churches were built on these sites.

From 138-325 AD, most all believers struggled to understand how Jesus was both God and man. Yet as the Nazarene believers became increasingly isolated from their Gentile brothers, they also became more confused in the focus of their worship and practice of their faith. From the fourth to the eighth centuries, edict after edict was passed to destroy the Jews including the Nazarene believers. Jews were hated as Christ killers and the only way a Jew could save his life was not only to believe in Jesus but also to reject all forms of Jewish life and traditions such as keeping the Sabbath, observing Passover, the Old Testament feasts, circumcision, etc. So the Jewish believer and the Nazarene had to totally deny their Jewishness to survive. This persecution increased through the thirteenth century, culminating in the Inquisition and the Crusades. The identity of Christian Jews began to disappear with their assimilation of believing Jews into the Roman Church either by force or by choice. Most gave up their Jewish cultural practices simply to survive. The Jews were increasingly viewed as cursed by God and all their blessings had now passed upon the Church which now had replaced Israel. These notable Jewish believers came under the authority of the church, no longer having a Jewish identity.

The Reformation slowly began to change the view of believing Christians toward the Jews, and with that change came a work of God's grace. Previous to the Reformation, Christians viewed the Old Testament law as opposed to Christian faith. But the Reformers taught that Christ's life fulfilled all Old Testament law for Christians and believers ·

were also to obey the law of God. As early as 1573, the Bishop of London proclaimed, "the judicial laws of Moses are binding on Christians and they ought not in the slightest degree to depart from them."[1] Instead of persecuting Jews, the Puritans saw the Jew as a mission field and Oliver Cromwell in the 17th century invited the Jews to England in hopes of their conversion. A treatise written in 1621 expresses this vision in its, "<u>The World's Great Restoration or Calling of the Jews and With Them All Nations and Kingdoms of the Earth to the Faith of Christ</u>."

The Puritans of 17th century England identified strongly with the persecuted Jews. In 1649, Joanne and Ebenezer Cartwright petitioned the English government.[2] Hebrew became a popular part of classical learning and by 1644 the Church of England required all candidates for the gospel ministry in England to learn Hebrew.[3] The first Hebrew translation of the New Testament appeared in 1817 and after three centuries of Reformation, the Reformed churches were committed to actively evangelizing the Jews. Founded in 1808, the London Society for Promoting Christianity among the Jews was established with great hopes of evangelizing the Jews and the world. Thirty years later 207 Jews believed in Jesus in England. The society was often ridiculed as foolish and Utopian. One man tried to prove his wife insane before the Lunacy Commission by exposing her hope in the conversion of the Jews as demonstrated by her membership in the "Jews society." He said, "Are you aware, my lord, that she subscribes to the society for the conversion of the Jews?" The chairman of the commission, Lord Shaftesbury, responded by saying, "Are you aware that I am president of that Society?" It was Shaftesbury's vision to start the "Jews society" to evangelize Jewish people (p. 187, Tuchman)

The Free Church of Scotland sent R. M. McCheyne and Andrew Bonar on a mission in 1839 to find out how many Jews there were and where they lived in Jerusalem and Palestine, Europe, Turkey, Austria, and Germany and what would be necessary to evangelize them. All this was in response to the Reformation vision of the 1560 Geneva Bible's comment on Romans 11:15, 26 that God shows "that the time shall come that the whole nation of the Jews, though not every one particularly, shall be joined to the church of Christ." This paved the way for Jewish Christianity to become a new spiritual community. As Hugh Schonfield acknowledges:

> It must be clearly recognized, however, that the Missions to the Jews, mainly founded in the nineteenth century, paved the way directly for the reconstitution of Jewish Christianity as an organic spiritual community, not only because their high-souled efforts won thousands of Jews for Christ and so provided the living materials for such a reconstitution, but because some of them sponsored and assisted the first hesitant steps of Jewish Christians to unite with one another in a corporate existence. The debt of Jewish Christianity to the modern Protestant missions is indeed an overwhelming one, and can only be repaid by the fullest exhibition of Christian character and by the utmost endeavour to realize in function the vision of so many saintly Gentile Christians of a national Jewish witness for Jesus the Messiah that in the dark hour of almost universal unbelief would hold aloft the torch of faith, and fulfill the historic mission of Israel to the world by showing forth the pattern of a kingdom of priests and a holy nation.[4]

By 1876 the author George Eliot wrote a novel that was popular among the English people entitled Daniel Deronda. The book, although unknown now, was probably the most influential book of the 19th century. The book gave expression to Zionist hopes that, "The world will gain as Israel gains." The hopes for the Jewish people peaked at this point, resulting in an even greater missionary zeal for the Jews in Israel.

On October 5, 1841, Michael Solomon Alexander, a Jewish believer, was appointed the Anglican Bishop of Jerusalem with approval by Queen Victoria. When he prematurely died in 1845, thirty-one believing Jews testified:

> Next to yourself and your dear family, we consider ourselves the chief mourners; for we feel both collectively and individually that we have lost not only a true Father in Christ, but also a loving brother and a most kind friend. The suavity and benignity of his manner, which so greatly endeared him to all, and which gained him the highest and most entire filial confidence of every one of us, tend much to increase the keen sense we feel of our loss. The affectionate love he bore to Israel, which peculiarly characterized him, could not fail to render him beloved by every one who had the privilege of being acquainted with him; while his exalted piety, and most exemplary life and conversation, inspired the highest reverential esteem. He was a burning and a shining light; and when he was raised to the highest dignity in the church, he conferred the most conspicuous honor on our whole nation, but especially on the little band of Jewish believers. With him captive Judah's brightest earthly star has set, and the top stone has been taken away from the rising Hebrew Church.[5]

O that all Jews would confess Jesus with the clarity of the Hebrew Christian David Baron:

> What we continually press upon the Jews is that we believe in Christ as the Son of Man and Son of God, *not in spite of, but because we are, Jews.* We believe that Jesus is the Divine King of our people, the sum and substance of our Scriptures, the fulfiller of our Law and our Prophets, the embodiment of all the promises of our covenant. *Our testimony is that of Jews to Jews.*[6]

Hebrew Christian societies were established in England and throughout Europe to encourage Jewish believers to live out their lives as both Jews and believers.

Joseph Rabinowitz, after a trip to Jerusalem in which he came to believe that the only hope of Israel "is in the hands of our brother Jesus," (The History of Jewish Christianity, Hugh J. Schonfield, p. 224, Kemp Hall Press, Ltd., 1936) established the Hebrew Christian Alliance.

As a result of these witnesses raised up in our Savior's name, thousands of Jews throughout Europe and Russia came to faith in Jesus as their Messiah. The testimony of Rabbi I. Lichtenstein must thrill every believing heart:

> A sudden glory, a light, flashed through my soul. I looked for thorns, and fathered roses; I discovered pearls instead of pebbles; instead of hatred, love; instead of vengeance, forgiveness; instead of bondage, freedom; instead of pride, humility; instead of enmity, conciliation; instead of death, life, salvation, resurrection, and heavenly treasure.[7]

If God could save Rabinowitz and Lichtenstein, could it not be possible that millions of Jews will yet give the same testimony that Jesus Christ is the Messiah?

The first World War swept away ghettos as well as dynasties and gave new freedom to the gospel among the Jews. After the war, 97,000 Jews joined the church in Hungary, 17,000 in Austria, 35,000 in Poland, 60,000 in Russia, and 20,000 in America.[8] Although these are small numbers in contrast to the total Jewish population nonetheless, the dream of "all Israel being saved" has much greater credibility today than in 1839. If God can save a few, He will someday save "all."

God has preserved the Jews as a witness to His sovereign grace. We have yet to see the complete fulfillment of our God's promise in Romans 11:26.

Chapter 6

Preparation for the Fulfillment of the Dream

The Borders of Israel

For generations, from the time of the Reformation until 1900, the prayer of godly Christians was for "the peace of Jerusalem" and for the gospel to prosper among the Jews. The father of British General Edmund Allenby faithfully prayed for God's blessing of the gospel to the Jews. He never imagined that God would choose his own son to significantly further the ministry of the gospel among the Jews. By December 11, 1917, General Allenby had defeated the Ottoman Turks throughout Palestine, and took control of Jerusalem for Great Britain without having fired a single shot. The change of authority in Jerusalem came after 1000 years of Muslim domination. The British victory over the Turks and authority over the land of Palestine intensified the hope of Jewish people for a Jewish homeland. Thirty-one years later, on November 29, 1947, the United Nations voted to grant Israel the status of a nation. On May 14, 1948 a British major gave the key to the Jerusalem's Zion Gate to an elderly Rabbi Mordechai. When the Romans destroyed Jerusalem, the despairing priests threw the keys to heaven crying, "God henceforth be Thou the guardian of the keys." Time reported on August 16, 1948 that "out of the concentration camps, ghettoes, courtrooms, theaters and factories of Europe had assembled the Jewish people and they had won their first great military victory since 160 BC. Israel's victory came after the worst of a thousand persecutions."

The vision from God's Word that began with the Reformers and continued on by the godly hopes of the

Puritans and acted upon most fully by the Scottish and British missionaries of the 19th century was now in full bloom in the hearts of the Jews themselves. These events were interpreted by the Jews at the time as a fulfillment of Old Testament prophecies creating in them a desire to fulfill even more prophecies. The discovery of the Dead Sea Scrolls in 1948 and particularly of the Isaiah scroll now enshrined in the Israel Museum gave a greater sense of fulfilling their God-given destiny. Prophetic hopes soared amongst Bible-believing, evangelical Christians as they stimulated and encouraged Jewish hopes for their own homeland. Christians saw Israel's "establishment as a nation" as a powerful sign of God's love for the Jews.

Indeed, Israel's reestablishment and reunification of Jerusalem during the Six Day War was such an amazing event that it could only come from the hand of God. The Council of Thirteen, which was the provisional government of Israel, barely accepted the UN's invitation to become the state of Israel in a 5 to 4 vote. United States Secretary of State Marshall urged the Council to vote against nationhood out of fear of war with the Arabs.[1] On May 14, 1948, Prime Minister David Ben Gurion announced after the Hebrew blessing, "'Blessed art Thou O Lord, our God, King of the universe, who has kept us alive and preserved us and enabled us to reach this season,' that the state of Israel has arisen."

The weapons Israel desperately needed in order to defeat the Arabs came from Czechoslovakia, then a Communist-controlled country, not from England or the USA, their staunchest allies. Their greatest military victory came in the Six Day War in June of 1967. While they were fighting against Egypt, Israel pled with Jordan to remain neutral. But Jordan insisted on entering the war only to lose Jerusalem totally to Israeli control. It was shocking to see the ease with which the Israelis took Jerusalem. Certainly the hand of God was with this new nation! Even the Israelis were shocked at their own efficiency in defending and extending their borders. Yet the re-establishment of this nation prefigured something greater.

"It shall come to pass in that day that the Lord shall set His hand a second time to recover the remnant of His people who are left. He will raise a banner for the nations and gather the exiles and will assemble the outcasts of Israel and gather together the dispersed of Judah from the four corners of the earth." (Isaiah 11:11-12)

As Israel established and expanded her borders, Jews returned to Israel from all over the globe. To many it was a return from exile reminiscent of Israel's return from the Babylonian Captivity. Yet, this second return from exile is distinguished in all the history of Israel because this gathering brings the people of Judah back from the four corners of the earth.

God promised that when all the blessings and curses are fulfilled that

"the Lord God will bring you back from captivity and have compassion on you and gather you from all the nations again where the Lord your God has scattered you... Then the Lord your God will bring you to the land which your father possessed and you shall possess it." (Deuteronomy 30:3, 5)

In May of 1948, Israel was a country of 600,000. Today it has prospered to a population of over ten times that size, drawing Jews who had been dispersed all around the globe and especially to the north. God said *"I will say to the north give them up"* (Isaiah 43:6). From 1948 until 1964, 223,000 Jews returned to Israel from Poland and Romania. Between 1989 and 1996, over 700,000 Jews immigrated to Israel from Russia. David Baron, the head of the Liaison Bureau in Israel said, "I believe that the Russian immigration in the past five years is a greater miracle than all the miracles that have happened since the state of Israel's founding including the Six Day War."

These verses could not apply to the return from the first exile because that return was from the eastern nations of Babylon and Persia.

Was God's promise in Isaiah 43:6 fulfilled by the return from Babylonian exile?, *"I will say. . . to the south 'Do not keep them back. Bring my sons from afar and my daughters from the ends of the earth.'"* On January 4, 1985 Operation Moses airlifted 15,000 Falashas from the Marxist government in Ethiopia. We have witnessed the fulfillment of Ezekiel 34:28-30:

> *"'And they shall no longer be a prey for the nations, nor shall beasts of the land devour them; but they shall dwell safely, and no one shall make them afraid. I will raise up for them a garden of renown, and they shall no longer be consumed with hunger in the land, nor bear the shame of the Gentiles anymore. Thus they shall know that I, the Lord their God, am with them, and they, the house of Israel are my people, says the Lord God."*

Did God accomplish this return from exile in the sixth century BC or did He accomplish it after 1948 to the present? To ignore the dramatic nature of this return in the twentieth century is to rob God of His sovereign work in history.

> *"I will build you and you shall be rebuilt, O virgin of Israel! For thus says the Lord: 'Sing with gladness for Jacob, and shout among the chief of the nations; Proclaim, give praise, and say, "O Lord, save Your people, the remnant of Israel!" Behold, I will bring them from the north country, and gather them from the ends of the earth, among them the blind and the lame' . . . Hear the word of the Lord, O nations, and declare it in the isles afar off, and say, "He who*

scattered Israel will gather him, and keep him as a shepherd does His flock."" (Jeremiah 31:4-11)

This immigrant people has rebuilt the country according to the prophecy of Isaiah 61:4, *"They will rebuild the ancient ruins and restore the places long devastated, they will renew the ruined cities that have been devastated for generations."* Seemingly overnight, cities such as Ashdod and Ashkelon have been rebuilt. High-rise apartment buildings now tower over the Mediterranean Sea and boulevards make the cities look like Brooklyn. Cities such as Mitzpah Ramon are growing and thriving. Cities built on ancient sites from Bible times that have been dormant for centuries are now thriving centers of life and commerce. The Israeli Department of Antiquities is doing archaeological work and rediscovering the rich Biblical heritage of the country. In turn, Bible scholars are learning about such cities as Sepphoris, only recently discovered in 1991 and opened as a national park in 1995. The country described as barren by Mark Twain in 1869 is now blossoming. The Word of God has been fulfilled before our materialistic eyes. *"And it shall come to pass that as I watched over them to pluck up, to break down, to throw down, to destroy, to afflict, so I will watch over them to build and to plant"* (Jeremiah 31:28). Jewish life and culture that were on the verge of extinction 50 years ago is being reborn.

Circumcision of the Heart

God couples promises to Jews for their land together with the promises of spiritual revival. For example, in Deuteronomy 30:6 God says, *"And the Lord your God will circumcise your heart and the heart of your descendants, to love the Lord your God with all your heart and with all your soul, that you may live."* When God breaks the yoke of foreigners in that day, *"they shall serve the Lord their God, and David their king, whom I will raise up for them"* (Jeremiah 30:9, cf. Hosea 3:5).

As attested to in Nehemiah, Haggai, and Zechariah, the return from the Babylonian exile did not result in submissive worship and obedience as promised in these verses. Selfishness crippled community spirit as the returned exiles focused on their personal homes rather than the rebuilding of the temple (Haggai 1:9). *"'I struck you with blight and mildew and hail in all the labors of your hands; yet you did not turn to Me,' says the Lord"* (Haggai 2:17). Zechariah pleaded with the Lord's people not to continue in the same sins that resulted in the destruction of Jerusalem, the nation, and the exile (Zechariah 1:3-6).

> *"Then the word of the LORD came to Zechariah, saying, 'Thus says the LORD of hosts: Execute true justice, show mercy and compassion everyone to his brother.' Do not oppress the widow or the fatherless, the alien or the poor. Let none of you plan evil in his heart against his brother.' But they refused to heed, shrugged their shoulders, and stopped their ears so that they could not hear. Yes, they made their hearts like flint, refusing to hear the law and the words which the Lord of hosts had sent by His Spirit through the former prophets."* (Zechariah 7:8-12)

The first return from exile did not result in the nation of Israel repenting and turning to the Lord (the circumcision of the heart prophesied in Deuteronomy 30:6). But the return resulted in the Jewish people united as a nation so that they were in a position to receive the Messiah Jesus. *"But having come to His own they did not receive Him"* (John 1:11). This second return to the land is a call for the Jewish people to repent and receive their Messiah as their Savior and King.

What Does It Mean to be Jewish?

Although the physical land is important in the reassembling of the Jews, we must see that the existence of

. this State of Israel is not essential to the revival of the Jews. God promises salvation in the land, not purely possession of the land. They inherited the land according to God's promise, *"Blessed are the meek for they shall inherit the earth"* (Matthew 5:5). The Israeli government, seeking to be genuinely democratic, has attempted to involve the Arabs, who are predominantly Muslims in their government. Yet the religious character of the government is a complex and confusing question that still hangs over the entire nation. The nation has not really answered the question, "What does it mean to be Jewish?" First, is Jewish religion important? The nation was established as a secular nation. Yet the Orthodox are seeking to define the character of the nation putting them in conflict with secular Jews.

Other questions also arise. Who can come to Israel under the Law of Return? What is the ideological and theological vision for the nation? The answer to the question, "What does it mean to be Jewish?" will deeply affect the future of Israel. Jewish people from all over the world have their eyes on Israel and have a definite interest in what takes place in the country.

What should Christians think about these events of history? It is important to understand that the promises of God are not linked with the government of Israel or with a unified Jerusalem. Those evangelical believers who support the government of Israel, right or wrong, are refusing to fulfill the prophetic role to the Jewish people to call them to repentance toward God and faith in Jesus as Messiah. Our vision is not so simple as to stop at a politically unified Jerusalem. Our vision is for a spiritually unified Jerusalem washed from their sin, destroying the idols of the city and walking in joyful obedience to the righteous law of God. The land is important to the revival, but not necessarily as the State exists today.

Some evangelical leaders insist on the State of Israel reclaiming all of the land, including Gaza and the West

Bank, in their nation. The State of Israel is reluctant for political reasons. The recent withdrawal from Gaza and the United States government's support of Israel in this action has resulted in some evangelical leaders asserting that Hurricane Katrina devastated the Gulf States of the United States on the U.S. government's support of Israel's withdrawal from the Gaza. This is a misdirected concern. The concern is that "all Israel is saved" (Romans 11:26). God will give the land to those who meekly submit to Christ's rule and reign and receive His righteousness (Romans 10:3-4). Someday the entire land including Syria down to Egypt will be filled with those who worship the Father in Spirit and in Truth (John 4:23).

"In that day there will be highway from Egypt to Assyria, and the Assyrian will come into Egypt, and the Egyptians will serve with the Assyrians. In that day Israel will be one of three with Egypt and Assyria, even a blessing in the midst of the land, whom the Lord of hosts shall bless, saying, 'Blessed is Egypt My people, and Assyria the work of My hands, and Israel My inheritance.'" (Isaiah 19:23-25)

If genuine peace is to come to Israel, the faith of the nation will need to be clearly defined on the basis of Biblical truth. God is able to open a fountain for the house of David and for the inhabitants of Jerusalem (Zechariah 12:1-2) without Jerusalem being under Israeli rule. The events of 1917, 1948 and 1967 focus our attention on Israel, but we must be modest about our claims for Israeli control over the land, and especially over Jerusalem as we pray for the peace of Jerusalem. We long for the revival knowing that the final character of the nation is yet to be determined.

God has often used nations to further His plans and purposes. In the case of Israel, revival does not depend upon the nation we know as Israel today. The secular Jews that flaunt God's law must remember that the land they live in "spews out" those people who defy God's law (Deuteronomy

11:17). Possibly such an insistence upon Israeli rule over a unified Jerusalem will result in the nations gathering to do battle against Jerusalem (Zechariah 14:2). Yet the hope of the Jews coming in vast numbers to the Messiah is a realistic dream that requires the energies and prayers of the Church to fulfill. We must be modest in our dreams about the state of Israel and our eschatological expectations regarding the future of an earthly Jerusalem, the place from which the law goes forth and where all nations will come to worship at the mountain of the Lord (Isaiah 2:2-4). Such passages may very well be referring to the heavenly Jerusalem in Hebrews 12:22 rather than an earthly Jerusalem. Nevertheless, we must minister the gospel to the Jewish people without clear answers to the question of the place of the State of Israel in Biblical prophecy and the connection between the earthly and heavenly Jerusalem. Our only confidence is that God will revive His people to faith in the Messiah, Jesus. Today is the day of salvation for the Jewish people. They must be called to repentance today. The nations will be blessed as "all Israel" is saved.

Chapter 7

The Land and the Arabs

Israel is viewed by many professing Christians (and even by those who are merely curious about the future) as the key predictor of what will happen in the future. Interest has skyrocketed in "prophecy," and it does not seem to matter whether such interpreters of prophecy are even remotely close to accurate in their predictions of the future - people still love to speculate about the future. The return of the Jews, statehood for Israel in 1948, and the 1967 war all seem to indicate that the end of the world must be near. Yet such speculation is closer to fortune-telling than to Biblical prophecy. The Bible teaches that the "testimony of Jesus is the spirit of prophecy" (Revelation 19:10).   Speculation regarding prophecy is ungodly if there is no zeal to minister the gospel of Jesus Christ to the Jews. Why is there so little effort made to evangelize the Jewish people by these prophetic teachers?   One would think that the study of prophecy would motivate Christians to evangelize the Jews. But, sadly, while Evangelicals commit themselves to supporting the State of Israel, raising money to fly Russian-Jews to Israel, or celebrating Succoth in Jerusalem, very little effort is made to minister the hope of the gospel to Jewish people. Some are afraid to offend them. But, if Jesus is the way, the truth and the life, to refuse to offer freely the gospel because of fear of offending is blatant anti-Semitism. Such fear is prejudicial. God will save Jewish people as He did in the book of Acts. We are called to be faithful, but present day prophetic speculation sidetracks such gospel ministry.

Focus on Jewish issues such as the unity of Jerusalem, the borders of the land, etc., also takes away the responsibility to minister the gospel to the Arabs and

Palestinians. They, too, need the gospel. *"The testimony of Jesus is the spirit of prophecy"* (Revelation 19:10).

The Land of Promise to Abraham has a great spiritual meaning that extends beyond political boundaries and historical contentions. *"The earth is the Lord's and the fullness of the land"* (Psalm 24:1). The purpose of the land is that *"the righteous shall inherit the land and dwell in it forever."* Abraham was promised the land but was not allowed to possess it because the iniquity of the Amorites was not yet full. (Genesis 15:16) When the iniquity of the Canaanites was considered ready for judgment, then God sent the children of Israel in to judge them. Jacob experienced the land as the gateway to heaven when he envisioned the ladder coming down from heaven at Bethel (Genesis 28:17). Joseph wanted to be buried in the Land of Promise because it was the gateway to heaven (Genesis 50:25).

Some theologians would see the land as having no significance today. Yet we must ask, why would God have the Jews return to this land unless He was calling them to repent of their iniquities and live righteously in the land? From this land will flow the blessing of the Lord: *"You shall no longer be termed Forsaken, nor shall your land any more be termed Desolate; . . . for the Lord delights in you . . ."* (Isaiah 62:4). Jerusalem is to become a praise in all the earth as a city of praise. The nations will come to Jerusalem to learn how to keep the law of God. *"Come and let us go up to the mountain of the Lord to the house of the God of Jacob; He will teach us His ways and we shall walk in His paths for out of Zion shall go forth the law and the word of the Lord from Jerusalem"* (Isaiah 2:3).

"In that day the Branch of the LORD shall be beautiful and glorious; and the fruit of the earth shall be excellent and appealing for those of Israel who have escaped. And it shall come to pass that he who is left in Zion and he who remains in Jerusalem will

be called holy; everyone who is recorded among the living in Jerusalem. When the Lord has washed away the filth of the daughters of Zion, and purged the blood of Jerusalem from her midst, by the spirit of judgment and by the spirit of burning, then the LORD will create above every dwelling place of Mount Zion, and above her assemblies, a cloud and smoke by day and the shining of a flaming fire by night. For over all the glory there will be a covering." (Isaiah 4:2-5)

Are these references to Zion and Jerusalem focused on the earthly Zion and Jerusalem? Clearly, in passages such as Galatians 4:24, Paul identifies the earthly Jerusalem as those who attempt to keep the law of God as a means of justifying oneself. The heavenly Jerusalem is inhabited by those who receive the gospel promises. The heavenly Jerusalem is free because of God's covenant of grace through Sarah and her son Isaac. The earthly Jerusalem is enslaved like Hagar and her son Ishmael. Further, in Hebrews 12:22 true worshippers of our Lord Jesus are those who come to Mount Zion and the heavenly Jerusalem,

"to an innumerable company of angels, to the general assembly and church of the first born who are registered in heaven, to God the Judge of all, to the spirits of just men made perfect, to Jesus the Mediator of the new covenant." (Hebrews 12:22-24)

Jesus as the Son of David rules on the throne of David in power as He pours out the Holy Spirit to save:

"Men and brethren, let me speak freely to you of the patriarch David, that he is both dead and buried, and his tomb is with us to this day. Therefore, being a prophet, and knowing that God had sworn with an oath to him that of the fruit of his body, according to the flesh, He would raise up the Christ to sit on his throne, he, foreseeing this, spoke concerning the resurrection of the Christ, that His soul was not left

in Hades, nor did His flesh see corruption. This Jesus God has raised up, of which we are all witnesses. "Therefore being exalted to the right hand of God, and having received from the Father the promise of the Holy Spirit, He poured out this which you now see and hear. For David did not ascend into the heavens, but he says himself: 'The LORD said to my Lord, Sit at My right hand, till I make Your enemies Your footstool. Therefore let all the house of Israel know assuredly that God has made this Jesus, whom you crucified, both Lord and Christ. " (Acts 2:29-36)

The terms *Zion* and *Jerusalem* do in some cases refer to heavenly realities rather than physical realities. Yet, does the land have any ongoing significance in the light of how the Scriptures inter-relate the heavenly Zion and the earthly Jerusalem? If we understand the true spiritual character of the land, then we realize that the land is a sign intimately connected with these heavenly realities not in contrast and conflict with the heavenly realities. Zion and Jerusalem may refer back and forth between the two just as Paul moves back and forth between instruction regarding temporal marriage and teaching about Christ and the Church in Ephesians 5:31 and 32. There is a spiritual connection where the earthly Zion and Jerusalem are intimately connected as a sign with the heavenly Jerusalem and Zion. For this, God in His Word can move easily back and forth between the earthly and heavenly locations because in reality they are one.

According to the Scriptures, the righteous will inherit the land. The land was the place for Israel to repent and love the Lord.

"Then the Lord your God will bring you to the land which your fathers possessed and you shall possess it. He will prosper you and multiply you more than your fathers. And the Lord your God will circumcise your heart and the heart of your descendants to love the

Lord your God with all your heart and with all your soul so that you may live." (Deuteronomy 30:5-6)

God has returned the Jews to their land for their repentance not merely for their pleasure and safety. If they refuse to repent than He is able to scatter them again as He did twice before and re-gather them a third time to fulfill these verses of covenant promise. The land is the place for repentance and a testimony to the nations. The land was so barren and desolate because of Israel's sin of rebellion against their covenant God, *"because they have forsaken the covenant of the Lord God of their father"* (Deuteronomy 29:25).

If the land is given by God to those who repent and trust Him, will the Living God give the land to the Palestinians? Is Islam a religion that honors God and His righteousness? Certainly not! God can use an unrighteous people to chasten His people until they repent. Such chastening and discipline is God's purpose for the Palestinians. Israel must grieve for their sins toward the eternal God before they will know the cleansing fountain of God's forgiveness and mercy. Are the Muslims righteous enough for God to give the land to them? Do they not worship a god of their own imagination and refuse to acknowledge the eternal character of God's Son and the righteousness provided in Jesus Christ? Indeed, Muslim attempts to establish their own righteousness instead of submitting to the righteousness of God is as hollow as Jewish efforts to establish their own righteousness (Romans 10:3). Righteousness is a gift. *"What shall I render to the Lord for all His benefits to me? I will take up the cup of salvation, and call upon the name of the Lord"* (Psalm 116:12). The psalmist asks what will he give and responds by taking the cup and calling on the name of the Lord. Giving to God in the case of forgiveness of sins and righteousness is to take the offer the Almighty so freely extends to us. *"This is the work of God, that you believe in Him who He sent"* (John 6:29). Muslims need the gospel of Jesus Christ. They need the cleansing of the blood of Jesus Christ to satisfy divine justice.

Those who repent, are cleansed of their sin and receive the righteousness God provided in Christ, will then inherit the land.

We dream of that day when Jews and Muslims in large numbers take the cup of salvation offered in Jesus Christ. The promise of God is that:

> *"There will be a highway from Egypt to Assyria and the Assyrian will come to Egypt and the Egyptian into Assyria and the Egyptians will serve with the Assyrians. In that day Israel will be one of three with Egypt and Assyria a blessing in the midst of the land, whom the Lord of hosts shall bless, saying 'Blessed in Egypt My people and Assyria, the work of My hands and Israel my inheritance.'"* (Isaiah 19:23-25)

This is the totality of all the land that was promised to Abraham in Genesis 15:18-21. The three nations stretch from the great river (the Nile) to the River Euphrates, thus fulfilling the promise to Abraham of being the "Promised Land". What was never accomplished by warfare will be accomplished by the rod of iron that Jesus wields through the gospel (Psalm 2). Only the gospel can break the heart hardened by sin and rebellion so that such a heart gladly worships the Father in heaven.

The repentance and faith of the house of David will overflow to the Arabs, formal Christians, Muslims and those from all over the world. Will not the end result be to cleanse the land of the idolatry that loudly proclaims God as Lord but in reality denies the truth of God's revelation? Is it possible that the "Christians" who worship in spirit and truth will tear down places of idolatry such as the Church of the Holy Sepulchre and the former Muslims who submit to the righteousness God provided in Christ will themselves tear down the Dome of the Rock (Zechariah 13:2). This cleansing of the land of idols will be the result of God's great work of salvation. The Temple Mount itself will be a genuine House of Prayer for all nations as Jesus proclaimed in Mark 11:17. The land is the place to offer genuine worship and to live before the Lord in righteousness. As Calvin comments on Zechariah 13:2, "God cannot be rightly worshipped except all corruptions inconsistent with his success and pure worship be taken away."

The current State of Israel exists to protect the people until the Jews repent and return to the Lord their God. Yes, the Jews need a place of protection for their national identity. This is God's purpose for the State of Israel. Zionists believed that "without a Jewish state there is no existence for the Jewish people." The state was established to protect Jewish heritage and identity. To the Jewish mind, to reject the Jewish claim to the land is tantamount to denying the Jews the right to exist as separate and distinct people. The Jewish State is built on the foundation of Rabbinic Judaism. Is this system of doctrine consistent with the Torah, which supposedly it is built upon? Jesus says the rabbinical tradition will be judged by Moses (John 5:45-47). If Judaism in fact is alien to the Scriptures and the character of God, then the entire foundation of the state must be repented of and changed. God calls for repentance because the peaceable fruit of righteousness cannot come from the root of a rebellious and lawless system of doctrine. The issues are interpretation of the Bible and theology, not merely government policy made through negotiation and compromise between warring factions. All we can hope for from the State of Israel, the Palestinian authority and those governments such as the United States that assist in the "peace process" is to provide outward peace. Such outward cessation of hostilities does allow the Church of Jesus Christ to minister the truth of the gospel and live it out before all the people of Israel so that they may repent and come to the Messiah, who can give life to a hopeless land. But a political peace will never result in Jerusalem being a praise in the earth. Only the gospel can bring peace to the city of peace, Jerusalem. Praying for the peace of Jerusalem means praying for the gospel to prosper and triumph in Jerusalem. The gospel alone is God's means of unifying Jerusalem.

To confront the people and the State of Israel for its sins in no way is to offend God. Prophetic confrontation like that of Elijah before Ahab in 1 Kings 17:1 is not to trouble Israel and expose oneself to the curse of Genesis 12:3 but is truly to love and bless Israel. So many Bible prophets today seem to teach that Jews are near to God by being Jews. Many think if we can get every Russian Jew to Israel they are closer to God. Just the opposite is true. As John the Baptist loudly proclaimed that God can raise up children of Abraham from rocks. Only the Jew who repents of his sin and trusts Jesus in His death and resurrection can be saved. Paul teaches in Romans 9 that not all Israel is Israel and that Jews need to be circumcised in their heart, not merely their flesh. Their praise must be from God not from men (Romans 2:28-29). The Almighty God of Abraham, Isaac, and Jacob will not indefinitely tolerate the rebellious disdain for the commands of Deuteronomy 6-26 by individuals or corporately by the State of Israel. Today is the day for Israel to grieve for their sins. We read of Josiah in 2 Chronicles 34:19 when King Josiah heard the words of the Law that he tore his clothes and returned to the Lord. If the Jewish people do not repent, God can drive them into the nations again and re-gather them a third time.

> *"Go inquire of the Lord for me, and for those left in Israel and Judah, concerning the words of the book that is found; for great is the wrath of the Lord that is poured out on us, because our fathers have not kept the word of the Lord, to do according to all that is written in this book."* (2 Chronicles 34:21)

Josiah truly repented and restored true worship in Israel. He is a model for leadership today. The repentance that God requires is to repent from the external worship of

Judaism. Judaism is not Jewish. Judaism is a form of rebellion against the Law of God as revealed in the Torah. Even the faith of the Jews is an idolatry that requires repentance and a submission to the Law of God. The promise of Jeremiah 31:31 is:

> *"Behold, the days are coming," says the LORD, "when I will make a new covenant with the house of Israel and with the house of Judah; not according to the covenant that I made with their fathers in the day that I took them by the hand to bring them out of the land of Egypt, My covenant which they broke, though I was a husband to them," says the LORD. "But this is the covenant that I will make with the house of Israel: After those days, says the LORD, I will put My law in their minds, and write it on their hearts; and I will be their God, and they shall be My people. No more shall every man teach his neighbor, and every man his brother, saying, 'Know the LORD,' for they all shall know Me, from the least of them to the greatest of them," says the LORD. "For I will forgive their iniquity, and their sin I will remember no more."*

The land will be inhabited by those who both worship at the heavenly Mount Zion and who live out righteousness as a corporate body before the nations of the world. The testimony of Jesus is to call people to repentance and faith. This is true prophecy. Speculation about the future is empty religion. Now is the time to minister the hope of the gospel to both Jews and Arabs. They will be a blessing to each other as they worship the Living God of Abraham, who is the father both of Isaac and Ishmael as well as their descendants.

Chapter 8

One Holy Temple

The Apostle Paul entered the Temple in Jerusalem in approximately 60 AD and was arrested by the Temple guard who also stirred up the whole crowd in the Temple. He was believed to have taken a Gentile past the Wall that separated Jews and Gentiles. If a Gentile went past that wall, then he would be subject to the death penalty. The Jews from Asia cried out: *"Men of Israel, Help! This is the man who teaches all men everywhere against the people, the law and this place; and furthermore he also brought Greeks into this place and defiled this place"* (Acts 21:28).

It is this wall that Paul writes about from prison, presumably in Caesarea, in Ephesians 2:11-21. Paul describes the Gentiles as being strangers to the covenants of promise and aliens from Israel, without hope and without God in this world.

"But now in Christ Jesus you who were far off have been brought near by the blood of Christ. For He Himself is our peace, who has made us both one and has broken down the middle wall of separation having abolished in His flesh the enmity, that is the law of commandments contained in ordinances, so as to create in Himself one new man from the two, thus making peace, and that He might reconcile them both to God in one body through the cross, thereby putting to death the enmity. And He came and preached peace to those who were afar off and to those who were near. For through Him we both have access by one Spirit to the Father. Now therefore, you are no longer strangers and foreigners, but fellow members of the household of God, having been built on the

foundation of the apostles and prophets, Jesus Christ Himself being the chief cornerstone, in whom the whole building being fitted together grows into an holy temple in the Lord in whom you also are being built together for a dwelling place of God in the Spirit."

Unity in Messiah

Paul pictures the tearing down of the wall in the Temple that separated Jews and Gentiles through the death of Christ on the cross and the building up of a new Temple that is spiritual rather than physical. Both Jews and Gentiles come to God the same way, by faith in Jesus Christ. Both Jews and Gentiles need to be given the gift of faith to call upon the Name of the Lord. Jesus Christ is the chief cornerstone. All must confess Him as the promised Messiah who fulfilled all righteousness and as the great High Priest He has offered Himself as an atonement for sin (Matthew 16: 16-19).

"For no other foundation can anyone lay than that which is laid, which is Jesus Christ...Do you not know that you are the temple of God and that the Spirit dwells in you? If anyone defiles the temple of God, God will destroy him. For the temple of God is holy, which temple you are." (I Corinthians 3:11, 16-17)

Jesus Himself is either the cornerstone or a stumbling stone to those who hear the gospel, as Peter asserts in 1 Peter 2:4-10. Those who believe on Jesus Christ are living stones being built up into a spiritual house, a holy priesthood, to offer up spiritual sacrifices acceptable to God through Jesus Christ.

Jewish people have had unusual opportunities in that they have a covenantal relationship to God as His chosen people. The Jews have been the custodians of the Word of God for centuries and they have a glorious heritage and history. God has made wonderful promises to the children of Israel. Most significantly, Jesus is a Messiah for the Jewish people and is descended from the Jews. Yet it is a blasphemy for Jewish people to assert that they are right with God simply because they are Jewish. Even some Gentile Bible teachers elevate the Jews above all peoples and imply that they are right with God by virtue of being Jewish. Jews must believe in Jesus to be right with God. They must come to Christ just the same way that Gentiles do. Jewish people are perishing without the gospel today and they need someone to proclaim the good news to them now.

There is only one body of believers in which there is no distinction between Jew and Gentile.

"For you are all sons of God through faith in Christ Jesus. For as many of you as were baptized into Christ have put on Christ. There is neither Jew nor Greek there is neither slave nor free, there is neither, male nor female; for you are all one in Christ Jesus. And if you are Christ's then you are Abraham's seed, and heirs according to the promise." (Galatians 3:26-29)

For this reason the Church is made up of both Jews and Gentiles and is the fulfillment of the promises made to Israel. Peter proclaims the Church to be

". . . a chosen generation, a royal priesthood, a holy nation His own special people that you may proclaim the praises of Him who called you out of darkness into His marvelous light; who were once not a people, but are now the people of God, who had obtained mercy but now have obtained mercy." (1 Peter 2:9-10)

These are the same descriptive terms God used for the children of Israel in Exodus 19:5-6. Paul speaks of this body of the Church as the Israel of God in Galatians 6:16. This hope does not replace Israel with the Church, but sees a new "assembly" in which both Jews and Gentiles are equal before

God through the work of Jesus Christ. Jews do not find their completeness in their "Jewishness"; Jews are complete in Christ who unites Jew and Gentile into an assembly called the church, content in its worship of the Triune God.

Yet equality before God in the manner of salvation between Jew and Gentile does not obliterate distinctions in God's plan for Jew and Gentile. Would anyone interpret Paul to be saying in Galatians 3:28 that the distinctions between men and women are now blotted out? No! Men have the responsibility for spiritual leadership in the home and the church and the role of women is that of nurturer and supporter. The callings of men and women are distinct even though equality of membership is assured in Christ. The reconciliation of Jew and Gentile through the broken body of Christ sacrificed on the cross allows both to come together into the presence of the Father. Both are built up into one holy temple in whom the Holy Spirit dwells (Ephesians 2:11-22). Such unity between Jew and Gentile in no way displaces the Jew but rather allows the Jewish people to fulfill the calling God purposed for them, to be a blessing to all the families of the earth (Genesis 12:3).

This one body which includes Gentiles as fellow heirs to the covenant promises is a mysterious fellowship, hidden until the time of Christ yet revealing the manifold wisdom of God (Ephesians 3:1-12).

Paul refers to the people of God as an olive tree in Romans 11:17-24. The original people of God were children of Abraham, the house of Israel. Paul refers to them in Romans 11 as the *"natural branches"* (Romans 11:21). Because of the Jews' rejection of Jesus as their Messiah, they became *"enemies of the Gospel"* (Romans 11:28). The Jewish people as a whole rejected Jesus as their Messiah and God cut off some of the branches of His chosen people (Romans 11:17). As a result of some Jews rejecting Jesus as their Messiah, Paul took the gospel to the Gentiles. Paul's mission given to him by God was as a chosen vessel of God to bear His name to the Gentiles. Paul magnified his office because his strategy was to minister the gospel to the Jews by reaching the Gentiles. When the synagogue rejected him, he then went to the Gentiles. Many in the synagogue rejected the gospel even as many Jews also believed. In reality, the Jews who were filled with envy contradicted and opposed the things spoken by Paul (Acts 13:45). The success of the gospel in the synagogue clearly ignited a reaction by those who resented the gospel Paul preached (Acts 13:46-57; 14:1-2). For example, at Corinth

"he reasoned in the synagogue every Sabbath, and persuaded both Jews and Greeks. When Silas and Timothy had come from Macedonia, Paul was compelled by the Spirit, and testified to the Jews that Jesus is the Christ. But when they opposed him and blasphemed, he shook his garments and said to them, 'your blood be upon your own heads: for I am clean. From now on I will go to the Gentiles.'" (Acts 18:4-6)

The Jews today who resist the truth as it is in the gospel of Jesus must acknowledge their own responsibility for their unbelief. Although the church has failed in many ways, the synagogue of the first century defined itself in reaction to the message of the gospel.

At the same time, usually overlooked by most New Testament interpreters is the huge success of the gospel among Jewish people in the first century. On the Day of Pentecost, three-thousand believed in Jesus and were baptized on Solomon's Porch on the stairs of the Temple. As a consequence, these Jewish believers continued daily in spiritual unity in the Temple, *"praising God and having favor with all the people. And the Lord added to the church daily those who were being saved"* (Acts 2:46-47). Five-thousand believed as a result of Peter and John's witness in the Temple (Acts 4:4). After the ordination of the first deacons in Acts 6:1-6, the testimony of the Scripture is,

"Then the word of God spread, and the number of the disciples multiplied greatly in Jerusalem, and a great many of the priests were obedient to the faith" (Acts 6:7).

As Paul began his ministry, he always began in the synagogue. On his first missionary journey, he went into the synagogue (Acts 13:14). After his sermon, *"many of the Jews and devout proselytes followed Paul and Barnabas, who speaking to them persuaded them to continue in the grace of God"* (Acts 13:44). However, there were those Jewish leaders who saw the multitudes gathering to hear the word of God who *"were filled with envy; and contradicting and blaspheming, they opposed the things spoken by Paul"* (Acts 13:45).

Again in Iconium, Paul preached in the synagogue of the Jews. *"A great multitude both of the Jews and of the Greeks believed. But the unbelieving Jews stirred up the Gentiles and poisoned their minds against the brethren"* (Acts 14:1-2). The success of the gospel in the synagogue clearly created a reaction by those who resented the gospel. Paul preached what was merely a testimony and witness of what he had received by revelation from Jesus Christ. Paul's gospel was the infallible ministry of the person and work of Jesus which was delivered to him.

Paul never willingly left the synagogue but only did so when forced out by the irrational envy and unbelief of those who threatened his life and rejected revealed Truth (Acts 13:46-51). He was expelled from the synagogue (Acts 13:50).

Paul likewise preached in Thessalonica in the synagogue of the Jews. Some of the Jews were persuaded (Acts 17:4), but again those who were not persuaded were *"becoming envious . . . , gathering a mob"* against Paul and Silas (Acts 17:5). In Corinth, Paul reasoned every Sabbath and "persuaded both Jews and Greeks" (Acts 18:4). Yet in every synagogue, Paul found opposition and blasphemy against his message that Jesus was the Christ and he was forced to leave the synagogue. Meanwhile, new "Nazarene" synagogues began developing within the land of Judah and in Galilee, and in the Diaspora "Christian" assemblies were developing made up of significant numbers of Jewish believers and Gentiles (Acts 11:26). This new faith was rooted in the worship and practices of the pre-Jesus synagogue that shaped the early church.

As a consequence, those who remained in the synagogue after expelling "the heretics" increasingly shaped and defined their existence in terms of being against their departed brethren and their faith in Jesus as Messiah. This unbelieving synagogue eliminated passages from synagogue worship that might give support to their "heretical" brethren for their interpretation regarding Jesus. Even the Decalogue was removed from the synagogue service as it was believed to give credibility to Jesus' claims. Between 80-90 AD at Javneh the *birkot ha minim* was declared upon Jewish believers (the Nazarenes) who were named as degenerates. These "heretics" were said to have followed their own hearts instead of the authoritative teachers of the Law. The "min" were considered worse than the Gentile heathen.

The synagogue retold the story of Jesus in the Tol'dot Jeshu in order to belittle Jesus by ascribing to him illegitimate birth, magic, and a shameful death. Because of this overall reaction to Paul, the preaching of the gospel, and the fact that so many Jews believed in Jesus, this significantly changed the character of the synagogue. The synagogue, which had existed partially as a means of maintaining Jewish identity but primarily as a place of learning the Torah and worship through Scripture study and prayer, was now used to identify what Judaism was not instead of providing a clear answer as to what Judaism is. Judaism came to be defined as not identifying with faith in Jesus. The first century synagogue increasingly became a place of self-protection rather than confident outreach influencing the world. The synagogue retreated out of fear and relied upon the weapons of social ostracism, religious excommunication and suppression. This guardian synagogue is the Judaism Paul had to deal with most frequently according to the Scriptures. While the reactionary synagogue retreated into tradition exclusively, the younger brothers, the Christians, grew in confidence and openness. *"These are they who have turned the world upside down"* (Acts 17:6).

Distinct Identity and Calling

Paul's confidence was, that by ministering the truth of the gospel to the Gentiles, ultimately the Jews would see the beauty of Jesus and His salvation, thereby coming to faith in Jesus as their Messiah. *"But through their fall, to provoke them* (the Jews) *to jealousy, salvation has come to the Gentiles"* (Romans 11:11). As a result of the Jews' fall, the blessing of the gospel went out to the Gentiles. Or, as Paul asserts in Romans 11:15, *"For if their being cast away is the reconciling of the world, what will their acceptance be but life from the dead?"* The Gentiles then are spoken of as being grafted into the olive tree which represents the "people of God." The olive tree is not a Jewish tree. The Jews are branches. Christ is the root and the people of God are the trunk. Unfortunately, many Jewish believers see the tree as their olive tree. But the danger is that Gentiles will boast against the Jews because the Church has become largely a Gentile Church. God warns against that kind of ethnic pride that forgets God's love and concern for His chosen people. *"Because of unbelief,, they were broken off, and you stand by faith. Do not be haughty but fear."* Paul urges the Gentiles to consider the *"goodness and severity of God . . ."* (Romans 11:22). The threat is that the Gentiles may be cut off as were the Jews. The Gentile Church may have lost its saltiness and may be swept away as good for nothing. We see entire areas of the world where the gospel once prospered and now they are totally Islamic with very little if any ministry of Christ's church, such as in Turkey and North Africa.

> *"For if you were cut out of the olive tree which is wild by nature, and were grafted contrary to nature into a cultivated olive tree, how much more will these, who are natural branches, be grafted into their own olive tree. And so all Israel will be saved."* (Romans 11: 24- 26)

This passage makes no sense unless Paul is speaking of ethnic Jews. Ethnic Jews are compared to ethnic Gentiles. Therefore Romans 11:26 indicates that God will keep a separate people called the Jews as an identifiable people group, and that identifiable people group will be saved in great numbers.

Application of this truth calls both Jews and Gentiles into one Church. There is to be no dividing the church into Messianic congregations based on race and Judaistic practices and Gentile congregations based on their cultural factors. Yet we also must free Jewish believers to keep Passover and Succoth and other Jewish traditions if they so desire. Gentiles likewise must consider their cultural practices imported into the church and refrain from offending Jewish believers in those practices. We are both called as Jews and Gentiles to the obedience of faith. The greatest testimony is that both Jews and Arabs and all Gentiles are able to be one church. Yet both may express cultural differences. For example, Jewish people are not required to keep those festivals God instituted in the Old Testament. But they should not be denied the privilege of observing God's festivals and practices. These are instructive to us all. Gentiles may freely enter into these celebrations. But the Jews and Gentiles are to worship together in the same church, not in separate congregations. The practices of the Church have been governed by the training received from the first Jewish disciples and are closer to the Jewish practice of the first century than those practices developed through Rabbinical Judaism since the destruction of the Temple.

The Reign of Messiah Over Jew and Gentile

Jesus as Messiah also rules over all people and all history. He holds the entire creation together.

> *"For by Him all things were created that are in heaven and that are on earth, visible and invisible, whether thrones or dominions or principalities or powers. All things were created by Him and for Him. And He is before all things, and in Him all things hold together."* (Colossians 1:16-17)

Jesus Christ "restrains and overcomes" all the enemies of the church for His own glory. Jesus is the "heir of all things" and upholds all things by the Word of His power (Hebrews 1:2-3). Daniel proclaims regarding the Son of Man:

> *"Then to Him was given dominion and glory and a kingdom, that all peoples nations and languages should serve Him. His dominion is an everlasting dominion which shall not pass away and His kingdom shall not be destroyed."* (Daniel 7:14)

One reason given by the Orthodox Jew for not believing in Jesus is that He did not usher in the kingdom. But Jesus Christ did bring in the kingdom. He is king, literally sitting on David's throne. He rules by the power of God's Word (Psalm 2). The kingdom is the power of the gospel which breaks apart our hard hearts like a "rod of iron" (Psalm, 2:9) and heals the heart that has been broken by the law of God (Psalm 107:20). All those who come under the authority of the Word of God are then gathered into Christ's kingdom which He calls the Church. As the Westminster Larger Catechism summarizes this truth: "Christ executes the office of king, in calling out of the world a people to himself, and giving them officers, laws, and censures, by which he visibly governs them…" (Larger Catechism Q. 45)

The Church is the kingdom of God come to the earth. On the confession of Jesus as the Son of the Living God who is our Redeemer and Messiah, Jesus states that He will build His kingdom and the gates of hell will not prevail against it. The keys of the kingdom are given to the Apostles in Matthew 16:19.

The Church is given the "keys of the kingdom" to preach the gospel and to examine the lives of those who profess faith in Jesus Christ. The Church is under Christ's authority and we are to disciple one another to grow in grace. Those who fall short of the standards Christ gives to us are to be admonished to repent and change their behavior. The ability to restore a brother who has offended is the evidence of maturity (Galatians 6:1). Therefore, the marks of a true Church of our Savior are the faithful preaching of the Word of God, the exercise of discipline and the proper administration of the sacraments of baptism and the Lord's Supper. Again as Daniel prophesies of the future:

"Then the kingdom and dominion, and the greatness of the kingdoms under the whole heaven, shall be given to the people the saints of the Most High. His kingdom is an everlasting kingdom and all dominions shall serve and obey Him." (Daniel 7:27)

Jesus is the Christ because He has ushered in such a kingdom as we read in Acts 2. Jesus is enthroned at the right of the Father. He is ruling on David's throne. The evidence of this rule is that the three thousand who believed and were baptized continued attending to the Apostle's Doctrine and the breaking of bread. They cared for one another's souls by meeting material needs. Yet they also met in homes to provoke each other to love and good works (Hebrews 10:25). This is indeed the kingdom of our Savior.

Jesus Christ is calling out a people to be His own special people to demonstrate His goodness and His virtues. There is only one "People of God" determined not by race but by faith in Jesus Christ. Yet distinctions among people groups are not obliterated. Around the throne of the Lamb we will see those who have been redeemed singing the same new song to the Lamb who is the Lion:

"You are worthy to take the scroll, and to open its seals; for you were slain, and have redeemed us to God by your blood out of every tribe and tongue and people and nation, and have made us kings and priests to our God; and we shall reign on the earth." (Revelation 5:9-10)

The Unified Praise of Diverse Peoples

Around that throne of Jesus, the children of Israel will gather with those from other people groups to sing this song of the Lamb. Their testimony will be that they were chosen by God not because of any other reason than that God loved them and called them His sons. In spite of being sustained by miracles, their repeated rebellion in the wilderness threatened their national existence (Numbers 14:11-19*). "When Israel was a child I loved him and out of Egypt I called my son. As they called them so they went from them; they sacrificed to Baals and burned incense to carved images"* (Hosea 11:1-2). Paul, in Romans 8, assures those who believe in Jesus Christ that they will never be separated from the love of Christ. Yet Paul is well aware that God had children who were disobedient and rebellious and who were "enemies of the gospel." Therefore in Romans chapters 9 through 11, Paul assures his readers that God has not forgotten His promises to Israel and in due time "all Israel will be saved" (Romans 11:26). Jeremiah acknowledges the horrific judgment upon Israel for their sins:

84

"your affliction is incurable, your wound is severe. There is no one to plead your cause, that you may be bound up; you have no healing medicine . . . For I have wounded you with the wound of an enemy, with the chastisement of a cruel one, for the multitude of your iniquities, because your sins have increased, I have done these things to you." (Jeremiah 30:12-15)

God goes so far as to call Israel "Lo Ammi," "not my people" in Hosea 1:9. We could collect passage after passage where God confronts Israel over their sin, culminating in God's threat of divorce from Israel.

Yet in spite of God's confrontation of Israel for sin and spiritual idolatry and adultery, He promises *"'For I am with you,' says the Lord 'to save you, yet I will not make a complete end of you. But I will correct you in justice, and will not let you go unpunished'"* (Jeremiah 30:11). Our Almighty God further promises: *"'And it shall come to pass, that as I have watched over them to pluck up, to break down to throw down, to destroy and to afflict so I will watch over them to build and to plant, says the Lord.'"* (Jeremiah 31:28) And why does God make such a promise? Is God schizophrenic and cannot make up His mind as to whether to punish or whether to show mercy on Israel? In no way does God assert that the Gentile Church "replaces" these promises to Israel, but He will sovereignly save "all Israel" (Romans 11:26).

God is absolutely consistent and persistent in ministering to His covenant people. The covenant of Exodus chapters 19 through 24 and Deuteronomy is based on the character of God. Israel's rebellion was no surprise to God. Dispensationalism historically has asserted that in spite of Jesus coming to His own, and the Jews not receiving Him that then the mystery period of the Gentile Church began as if this were "Plan B" in God's economy. The Ammillenialist tends to write off the Jews as having had their chance to receive the gospel and now the rest of the nations are to receive the gospel. Romans 1:16 is interpreted with the view that the Jews first heard the gospel. But having rejected Christ as a nation, they now must get in line with the other nations, because they have no special place in God's plan. God has "redirected" His promises as if those promises made with the Jews are a distant memory or worse yet forgotten. But the Jews are testimony that history is going some place.

The promises of God made to the Jews may be a distant memory to professing believers who are focused on their own interests rather than God's. But God never forgets His promises. He promised in Deuteronomy 30:5:

> *"Then the Lord your God will bring you to the land which your fathers possessed, and you shall possess it. He will prosper you and multiply you more than your fathers. And the Lord your God will circumcise your heart and the heart of your descendant, to love the Lord you God with all your heart and with all your soul, that you may live."*

How did God assure Israel for all generations that He would accomplish this but by calling heaven and earth as witnesses. For this reason Jeremiah the prophet writes:

> *"Thus says the Lord who gives the sun for a light by day the ordinances of the moon and the stars by night, who disturbs the sea, and its waves roar (The Lord of Hosts is His name): 'if those ordinances depart from before Me, says the Lord then the seed of Israel shall also cease from being a nation before Me forever.' Thus says the Lord: 'If heaven above can be measured, and the foundations of the earth searched out beneath I will also cast off all the seed of Israel for all that they have done, says the Lord'"*
(Jeremiah 31:35-37)

Further in Hosea 3:4-5 the Almighty promises:

> *"For the children of Israel shall abide many days without king or prince, without sacrifice or sacred*

pillar, without ephod or teraphim. Afterward the children of Israel shall return and seek the lord their God and David their King. They shall fear the Lord and His goodness in the latter days."

The Jewish people need David their king, that is, the one who rules on the throne of David as His Son yet also David's Lord (Matthew 22:41-45). The greatest need of the Jews is for the gospel. How can we lazily say that we do not owe a debt to the Jews who first ministered the gospel to the Gentiles? The Jews are assembled in their land and they need faithful witnesses of the power of God revealed in the cross of Jesus and in His resurrection power and glory to rule hearts through His Word. Do we question whether the gospel is powerful enough to save those who are most resistant to the gospel? Has the church lost confidence in the power of the gospel? Is that the real reason we will focus on every other nation and people group except the Jews? Woe to that prophetic preacher who assures a lethargic self-centered Gentile church that the Jews are closer to God by being Jewish and that God will save them after the secret rapture of His church. What is the purpose of flying Russian Jews to Israel where there is so little gospel witness? Why don't Christians spend their time and energies ministering the gospel to Jews whether they are in Russia or Israel? Why is it that we have millions of Jewish people assembled in Brooklyn, New York surrounded by Christian Churches who have a romantic view of the Jews but no urgency to care for them and love them by proclaiming the gospel to them for Jesus' sake? Is there no passion for building the one Temple described in Ephesians 2:21? *"Behold I am the Lord the God of all flesh. Is there anything too hard for Me?"* asks our God in Jeremiah 32:27. When God gathers His people He will cause them to dwell safely because:

"They shall be my people, and I will be their God, then I will give them one heart and one way, that they may fear Me forever, for the good of them and their children after them" (Jeremiah 32:38, 39). *"Behold*

87

the days are coming says the Lord that I will make a new covenant with the house of Israel and the house of Judah – not according to the covenant that I made with their fathers in the day that I took them by the hand to lead them out of the land of Egypt, My covenant which they broke though I was a husband to them says the Lord. But this is the covenant that I will make with the house of Israel after those days says the Lord : I will put my law into their minds and write it on their hearts ; and I will be their God and they shall be my people. No more shall every man say to his neighbor, and every man his brother saying 'Know the Lord' for they shall all know Me from the least of them to the greatest of them, says the Lord. For I will forgive their iniquity and their sin I shall remember no more. " (Jeremiah 31:31-34)

What is new about the New Covenant is not that the Covenant with Moses is now null and void but that the newness of the covenant is the person of Christ. He is the one who by His sacrifice as the great High priest has fulfilled the Old Covenant and by the power of the Holy Spirit is able to write the law upon the heart and give a new nature to fulfill it (see Hebrews 9:16-28). The Reformers understood that what made the difference between the Old and the New was the death of the testator. A legal will does not go into effect until the one who made the will dies. So the Reformers did not call the first 39 books of the Bible the Old Covenant and the 27 books written after Jesus the New Covenant but they called them the Old and New Testaments. The difference is in the administration, but the legal arrangements of the first are still valid. They are administered in a different manner.

Summary

The Lord God Almighty is building one holy Temple and all who believe are living stones in that Temple. In ˙

Ezekiel 40-47, the prophet pictures a huge temple that some think will be a literal temple built in the future. But Ezekiel pictures living water flowing out of the Holy of Holies for a healing to the nations. The water of the Holy Spirit flows from inside the Temple outside through the Holy Place into the Outer Court and toward the East down the mountain toward the Dead Sea. There is so much water that it fills up the Jordan Valley and runs into the Dead Sea.

> *"This water flows toward the eastern region, goes down the valley, and enters the sea. When it enters the sea, its waters are healed meaning they will no longer be salty where nothing can live. And it shall be that every living thing that moves, wherever the river go will live. There will be a very great multitude of fish, because these waters go there; for they will be healed, and everything will live wherever the river goes. It shall be that fishermen will stand by it in En Gedi to En Eglaim; they will be places for spreading their nets. Their fish will be of the same kinds as the fish of the Great Sea, exceedingly many."* (Ezekiel 47:8-10)

As they saw the great catch of fish from the Sea of Galilee, did not the Disciples understand what that Great High Priest of a new Temple commanded them: *"Follow Me and I will make you fishers of men"* (Matthew 4:19). *"Do not be afraid. From now on you will catch men"* (Luke 5:10). Jesus is the New Temple. We are built up into Him as Paul described in Ephesians 2:11-21. We are to be fishers of men starting with the Jews and going to every creature.

The bottom line is that today is the day of salvation for the Jews. Today they need the gospel. God has commanded us to make Jewish evangelism a priority. Will you obey? Or will you elicit all kinds of theological excuses to avoid God's clear command to go to the Jew first, and also to the Gentile? Is not the withholding of the gospel to the Jews the highest form of anti-Semitism?

Chapter 9

Choose You This Day

Speculation abounds in the world today as to when the next step in the "prophetic calendar" will take place. Who is the beast? Who is the anti-christ? When will the temple be rebuilt? The questions are endless. Yet the Bible asserts that "the spirit of prophecy is the testimony of Jesus." God calls us to repent and to come to Him for life. Revelation is not the prediction of events but the revelation of Jesus and His authority over all the nations. The cross of Jesus Christ is to be lifted up and exalted.

God commands His people to *"pray for the peace of Jerusalem"* (Psalm 122:6). Either we will pray for the gospel of peace in Jerusalem or Jerusalem will be a cup of trembling in our hands. What does it mean for us to "pray for the peace of Jerusalem?" Just as we pray for our daily bread and we still have responsibility to work for that bread, so praying for the peace of Jerusalem is more than simply praying, but must include acting on the promises of God. So how are we to respond to the promises of God? How do we demonstrate our confidence in the gospel as the power of God unto salvation to every one who believes, to the Jew first and also to the Gentile?

First, our primary responsibility is to examine ourselves as to whether we have personally grieved over our sins and called upon the Savior for cleansing. How can we call anyone to faith in Christ if we ourselves do not know God through His Son Jesus Christ? As we know God, our world grows larger by considering the needs of others and not just our own. Is a faith that is for our own personal welfare worthy of the Creator God who has redeemed us?

Second, we must come under the authority of Jesus Christ by submitting ourselves to Christ's Church. Professing Christians must repent of the self-centered attitude that refuses to be a meaningful part of a congregation that demonstrates the marks of the Church. These marks are the faithful preaching of the Word of God, the practice of discipline and the proper administration the sacraments. The Gentile churches responsibility is to be the kind of community that will be so attractive to Jewish people that they will desire their Savior.

Jewish communities are some of the most faithful communities in the world. Jewish people stand by one another in an unbelievable manner. How can Christians who continually fail to live out their lives in the covenant community of the church give testimony that the church's community life is to be desired? Believers in Jesus are one "holy nation" as Peter describes the church in 1 Peter 2:9. We must faithfully obey our Savior to build those kinds of communities that obey the commands of Scripture and provide a unified testimony to the Jewish people.

Third, the Gentile church must repent of attitudes of superiority to Jewish people. We must repent of any attitude that considers the Gentile church as not needing the Jews. We must repent of any thought that the promises of God to Israel are purely for the church and that they no longer apply to the Jews. We must acknowledge the debt that we owe to the Jews because the Jewish believers formed the foundations for the church today. Christian worship, if it is pure, is primarily based on Jewish practices of the synagogue. American culture does not ultimately define how the Christian life is to be lived. We must use Scripture to evaluate those practices that are purely cultural and be open to other cultures, including Jewish culture. Cultural practices are a means of expressing our faith. Our goal is to minister the Truth of God's Word as the color of water. You can mix many other substances with water. If you have a mixture such as coffee or tea already then you cannot mix other things with that mixture and it will still be palatable. We have the responsibility to keep the Truth free from unnecessary cultural additions.

Fourth, we must repent of attitudes that consider that the Jews do not need the gospel because God will save them without our ministry to them. The Jews are not saved because they are Jews. Nor are Jewish people closer to heaven because they are now in their land. Our faith is not in the Jews but is in the Lord. We must send qualified people to minister the gospel to the Jews. We must be prepared ourselves to minister the gospel to the Jews. Likewise, we must seek opportunities to evangelize the Jewish people no matter what the cost. The Gentile church needs to repent of not making Jewish evangelism a priority and take steps to correct that error.

Fifth, we must come alongside the congregations in Israel and assist them to fulfill their calling as a church. Congregations need to partner with other congregations to support them in their ministry. We can provide Bibles, written materials, children's materials and libraries for pastors and leaders. We can come alongside congregations and help them with outreaches into their neighborhoods. We can certainly pray and encourage the churches through letters and communications that they are important to us. The presence of Gentile believers in the congregations means a great deal to them. We do not want the congregation to cater to us as guests, but as guests, we are to take care of our own needs. Imagine how much time a guest can take of your time when they visit if they are not considerate. Remember how guests can keep you from fulfilling your responsibilities if they are not thoughtful to be of assistance to you.

Outsiders must not assume that they know the best way to help. Seek counsel from the congregations in Israel and listen to their needs. Be sure you are not creating problems that only harm the church in Israel instead of helping them.

One of the greatest needs is to help believers to establish small businesses. With the difficult time that the economy has experienced in Israel, there is a need for training men to become businessmen. Without small businessmen there is little financial support for the church to be able to grow. The most recent Russian immigrants who are so responsive to the gospel are the latest ones to arrive into the country and therefore are the first to be furloughed from jobs or to have their wages cut. They are suffering at this time and need help to become businessmen to support themselves, their families, and the church.

Sixth, we must assist with the training of leadership within the church in Israel. Pastors take up the role of pastoring spontaneously. In the past, those men who have interest in ministering the Word of God and caring for people become pastors, if they can develop a group or Bible study. These pastors are leaders who have never really had anyone train them. They are leaders by the call of God, but, temporarily speaking, they are leaders by default. Since the 1980's many churches have developed in Israel. Most pastors have no training and no evaluation as to their gifts and calling to serve as pastors. God has certainly provided faithful pastors for His people in Israel. But there are needs that have to be addressed for the future. As of 1999, almost no congregations had a doctrinal standard for their congregations. Teaching and preaching tend to be experientially oriented. This is understandable given the needs and the immaturity of the Church in Israel. Yet pastors and leaders need to see that the Church must stand on the Truth. The Church is the pillar and ground of the Truth (I Timothy 3:15). Jesus prayed in John 17:17, *"Sanctify them by Your truth, Your Word is truth."* The need is to see that there is such a thing as the *"whole counsel of God"* (Acts 20:27) and then as the system of truth Paul calls *"the pattern of sound words"* (II Tim 1:13). The faith is to be both reasoned and persuasive (Acts 19:8; Romans 6:17).

The expectation of so many believers is that some extraordinary experience will unite them rather than seeing that the faithful interpretation of the Scripture is essential to genuine unity. Experiential unity is only temporary. Pastors and leaders need to be trained in Biblical interpretation, Biblical and Systematic Theology and Historical Theology. They also need training in the skills of preaching, discipleship, counseling and the care of souls. There is very little opportunity in Israel for such training. At present, there are pastors and teachers from congregations outside the country who can and are assisting in this training. Should we not make our gifts available to the church in Israel?

Seventh, there is a need for processes for pastors to hold each other accountable for their ministries. If Truth is the foundation of the Church, then there need to be doctrinal standards to examine whether pastors and leaders are in accord with those Biblical standards. Does not the Lord hold pastors responsible for the content and the practice of that Truth? Consider how Paul held Peter accountable in Galatians 1 and 2. Acts 15 indicates that the assembly of pastors and elders are to deal with issues facing the church as a whole. The churches need assistance to deal with the various power and personality struggles that affect the entire body when unresolved. Congregations need training on how to be true peacemakers confronting differences rather than temporary peacekeepers that refuse to face differences either through avoidance or sentimental kindness.

Eighth, pastors need encouragement and assistance to know how to disciple those under their care. A church is an assembly under the authority of God's Word. Discipleship is expressed through the disciplines of learning to restore one another God's way as we are instructed in Matt 18:15-18 and Galatians 6:1. The Israeli culture encourages individuality and self-reliance. To learn to submit to one another in the fear of God as indicated in Ephesians 5:21 is not easy for many Israeli believers.

Yet, only as congregations grow as disciplined congregations, governing themselves to honor God by obeying God's commands, will there be the moral authority to give hope to a nation that has lost its way morally and spiritually. Congregations that are reconciled to one another, committed to discipling and disciplining one another, lay the foundation for a nation that is able to genuinely govern itself. Will God send forth His spirit to save "all Israel" before the leadership is in place to shepherd and disciple those new believers?

In the church, discipline is essential to the proper administration of the Lord's Supper. In I Corinthians 11:23-34, we are instructed to examine ourselves as to our life before our Lord. Are we honoring the Messiah or betraying Him? Like the disciples at the Last Supper, we are to ask ourselves, "Is it I" who is betraying my Savior? (Mark 14:19).

If we have offended a brother, then we are to leave our gift at the altar and first be reconciled to our brother and then return to worship (Matthew 5:23-24). The Lord's Supper is a witness that we are in communion with one another and with our Risen Savior.

The marks of the authoritative preaching of the Word, discipline, and the proper administration of the sacraments are essential to our visible God-honoring national church in Israel.

As of 1999, most congregations in Israel did not require baptism of professing believers. The majority of congregations lacked standards in administering communion. Few had a consistent process to examine those who took the Lord's Supper as to their profession of faith or walk with the Lord. Some administer the sacrament yearly in connection with a meal (Passover service) or possibly as part of a meal with traditional Jewish blessings. Some congregations limit the Lord's Supper to believers, but there is no unified practice for the congregations of Israel.

Generalizations of the church are very difficult, and these comments are not always applicable. The church is maturing and will continue to mature to increasingly demonstrate the Biblical marks of a God-honoring church. Yet praying for the peace of Jerusalem involves praying that the church in Israel will *"with one mind and one mouth glorify the God and Father of our Lord Jesus Christ"* (Romans 15:6). Through the unity of the church, *"the God of peace will crush Satan under your feet . . ."* (Romans 16:20).

Ninth, Gentile Christian churches need to assist the Israeli Church to gain greater freedom for ministering the gospel. The Israeli government is afraid of a free dialogue of ideas because the government has been high-jacked by a false system of doctrine known as Orthodox Judaism. This system of belief is primarily a system of behavior control that does not assist the people of its nation in self-control. The Orthodox hide behind groups that use government funding to squelch the free expression of ideas. On May 14, 1948 when David Ben Gurion declared the Independence of the State, he promised,

> "The State of Israel will be open to Jewish immigration and to the ingathering of the exiles. It will foster the development of the country for the benefit of all its inhabitants. It will be based on freedom, justice, and peace as envisioned by the prophets of Israel. It will ensure complete equality of social and political rights to all its inhabitants, irrespective of religion, race or sex. It will guarantee freedom of religion, conscience, language education and culture . . ."

How can the nation have freedom of religion if there is not true freedom to express all ideas of religion? What are the Orthodox so afraid of that they have to restrain open religious discussion? Their policies have led to some professing Jewish Christians being deported, while some seeking to bring the gospel to Israel have been detained at the airport and expelled from the country.

Tenth, the Jewish people are to be called to repentance for their national rejection of the prophets of Israel and their message of faith in Messiah who has come and fulfilled all of the prophetic vision. Likewise, the people who believe in the Orthodox Jewish system of thinking need to repent. But who will even make the effort to evangelize the Orthodox so that they have an alternative?

Eleventh, Jewish believers need to be discipled as to how to live a godly life loving the law of God. At the same time, there is a need to encourage and help Jewish believers to live out a Jewish life as a cultural and national identity. They have the freedom to maintain their own identify as Jews while recognizing that doing so in no way gives them greater justification before God.

Twelfth, Gentiles need to rediscover the Jewishness of the gospel. Studying the Jewishness of the gospel is equivalent to studying the historical background of the Old and New Testaments. A rejection of the Jewishness of the gospel is the equivalent of accepting Systematic Theology without a sufficient Biblical Theological base that studies the development of the revelation God has given to His people over time. If the State of Israel were dissolved, a great concern would be the protection of the archaeological sites. Some Palestinians have already gone on record that they want to promote their "history" to displace the Jewish people. What is Palestinian history? It is the worship of Baal and Ashtoreth and other gods. What is the history of the Palestinians? Some books are already debunking as myth the archaeological record that has given rise to the historical-grammatical method of Bible interpretation. The nineteenth century rise in interest in evangelizing the Jews was greatly fostered by an interest in the archeological record of "the Land" as it supported the historical account in the

Bible. The State of Israel has supported archeological study that has helped to expand our knowledge of Biblical times.

How will you respond to the Biblical command to "pray for the peace of Jerusalem"? Will the Gentile churches commit to ministering the gospel to the Jewish people? The promise of God is:

> *"'I will raise up the tabernacle of David, which has fallen down, and repair its damages; I will raise up its ruins and rebuild it as in the days of old; that they may possess the remnant of Edom, and all the Gentiles who are called by My name,' says the Lord who does this thing."* (Amos 9:11-12)

Our emphasis is on evangelizing the Jews because it is God's priority that a continuing mission to the Jews coincides with ongoing Gentile missions. As they repent and hope in the Messiah, God will give them peace with the Edomites (Arabs) who have historically been enemies. Repentance and cleansing begin with the Jews. Such a revival will bring life from the dead to the entire Middle East and to the nations (Romans 11:15). Will you respond to the call, believing the gospel is the power of God to the Jew first and also to the Gentiles?

Thirteenth, Palestinian and Jewish-believing congregations need support and encouragement to be reconciled with each other and to model for Israeli society what genuine unity Palestinians and Jews can have together.

Fourteenth, an eschatology based in the Scriptures needs to be developed and taught that considers both the Palestinians and the Jews. At present, two eschatologies have developed that polarize the two groups. This book is written as an attempt to give one eschatology that gives hope to both groups of people.

The Dream

The opportunity to evangelize the Jewish people is an open door before us as never before. Will you choose to commit yourself as Paul did to refuse to be ashamed of the gospel of Christ but believe the gospel is powerful to the Jew first and also the Gentile? Or will you permit yourself and the church to remain prideful and self-complacent, refusing to submit to our Savior's strategy of ministering to the Jews first? Will the church even be truly complete without the Jews becoming a substantial part of the church? Will our God give the world, your world, peace without ministering the gospel of peace to Jerusalem and the Jews?

Can we live with Israel's unbelief? Is Israel's unbelief a warning to the church of resting in temporal blessing rather than in the person of Jesus Christ? Is not the destiny of the church and Israel united together? Choose you this day!

Multitudes before us have dreamt of all Israel being saved and such a revival bringing blessing to the nations. That dream needs revival and given the emphasis that such a dream is given in the Bible. A response must be given by the Church and individual believers. Lethargic indifference will only result in God continually raising the stakes until He gets the world's attention. The fulfillment of the ancient promises to Abraham and Moses will be accomplished by God. History is going somewhere and is not merely drifting.

We must "pray for the peace of Jerusalem," realizing that all the eyes of the Jewish world, as well as the world as a whole, are on the city of Jerusalem and the land of Israel. Jerusalem is a mirror of the world. What happens in Jerusalem is like a stone thrown into the water that will have a ripple effect on the rest of the world. Jesus strategically told the disciples that when the Holy Spirit is come upon them then they will be witnesses in Jerusalem, Judea, Samaria and to the uttermost part of the world.

Come, let us dream together and join with those who are trusting God to do what may seem impossible – Jews, Palestinians, and those from all nations - worshipping the Father by honoring the Son as Savior and Redeemer. Our God loves to do the impossible! Amen!

Appendix

Come Now Let Us Reason Together:
A Plea to God's Chosen People

Over the past century, the Jewish people have found themselves the primary focus of three hostile totalitarian assaults upon their existence - German Nazism, Soviet Communism, and presently Islamism. These attempts at obliterating you as a people historically have elevated Jewish identity and sense of purpose. Yet the present crisis of terrorist attacks in Israel and growth of anti-Semitism worldwide have not stimulated a call for self-examination. Are the acts of terror purely random without meaning for Jews or for the world? If the world could be free from acts of terror, does that outward peace signify that all is right in the world?

Do Jewish people have a central place in history? What is that role and are Jewish people fulfilling their role? What connection does your suffering for centuries - from the ghettos to the Holocaust to the terror bombings - have for the future? Doesn't a nation have the responsibility if it is living under permanent siege to examine its moral standards and its reason for existence? Do not Jews living in the Diaspora have the obligation to also inspect their conduct and character, or should Jews live in moral complacency and spiritual lethargy, with consciences dulled by consumer abundance that views the terror with annoyed indifference? Does not such introspection at least require self-examination to inspire hope for the future?

Is not the God who promised to your father Abraham that He would make you a blessing to the nations of the earth still engaging you as a people? Can you continue to view your distress as purely an external threat - that if only these terrorists could be restrained and stopped - then everything would be "normal again"? Does God not have His eye on you in a special way, *"for he who touches you, touches the apple of His eye."* (Zechariah 2:8)? If the present distress of Jews in the State of Israel and the rising anti-Semitism throughout the world are not merely random meaningless events but are in fact under the authority of a sovereign Person who created the Jews as His chosen people who belong to Him as a historical witness, then such self-examination should be based on the promise God gave in His ancient Book, the Tenach, the Bible. To dismiss the Bible as irrelevant morally or spiritually is also to dismiss whatever historic claim Jewish people have to the land identified by the blue flag with the Star of David on it. You dismiss the Bible at your spiritual peril, with the perpetual expectation of continued terror until you "listen" to the Almighty who constituted you as a people.

Therefore, as the prophet Isaiah pleaded to the ancient State of Israel, so we plead, *"come now let us reason together"* (Isaiah 1:18). Today is a day of hope because the God of the Isaiah scroll promises,

> *"He has sent me to heal the brokenhearted, to proclaim liberty to the captives, and the opening of the prison to those who are bound; to proclaim the acceptable year of hope . . . to comfort those who mourn, to consoled those who mourn in Zion, to give them beauty for ashes, the oil of joy for mourning, the garment of praise for the spirit of heaviness . . ."*
> (Isaiah 61:1-3)

What people needs comfort more than your people? Who needs the spirit of heaviness and mourning to be lifted more than your people? Beauty and joy are offered to you, if you will but listen and respond to the One who created you as a people.

Today Jewish people view the greatest threat to their security to be outside of themselves – the terrorists, the bombings, the Palestinian Authority that protects terrorists, etc. In a similar manner, in the first century Jewish people saw the Romans and their taxes as the greatest oppression to themselves. Yet a Jewish Rabbi came proclaiming, *"Repent for the Kingdom of heaven is at hand."* The kingdom that first century Jews wanted was an external kingdom where Jewish people could control their identity and future without outside interference. From 164-63 BCE, the Jews had such a kingdom established by Simon Maccabee, which was expanded and sustained by subsequent Maccabean rulers. Jewish people looked for a Messiah who would conqueror, kill and control their outward circumstances so that peace, prosperity and freedom would be Israel's glory and heritage. But the Jewish people did not see that they personally needed to change. However, this prophet knew that the greatest threat was within the heart of Jewish people themselves rather than the threat of Roman overlords and taxes.

Freedom is experienced in righteous character, and peace is first internal before it can ever be established in the external world. Such character is defined as humility and poverty of spirit. The kingdom belongs to those who humble themselves. Again Isaiah teaches:

"For thus says the High and Lofty one who inhabits eternity, whose name is Holy: I dwell in the high and holy place and with him who has a contrite and humble spirit, to revive the spirit of the humble, and to revive the heart of the contrite ones." (Isaiah 57:15)

To such who are poor in spirit, they will enter the true kingdom. To the mourning, comfort is offered. To the meek, the land is your inheritance, yes, even Eretz Israel. Hungering and thirsting for righteousness is the route to satisfaction. Acting as a peacemaker results in being called a son of God. Our focus is moved away from outside problems to seeing the poverty of our own souls and how our character threatens our own peace and that of others. Jesus is not giving us a code of ethics or a check list to be crossed off but a vision for our character as a standard to evaluate ourselves. But in fact, do you not harbor hatred in your own heart for others or lust for what is not yours in your own imagination? You desire political treaties to "protect the peace." But do you even fulfill your own promises and is your word reliable? If you want freedom, serve your enemies. Go beyond what those who oppress you demand from you. Such self-examination will break through the business-as-usual complacency that both Jews in Israel and the Diaspora exhibit. Worse yet, some prefer escapism to self-evaluation? Jews in Israel are a people who live with daily fear that would unnerve most people. But they do so with a detached, matter-of-fact attitude that does not face their own death or their inability to protect those whom they love.

Why do Israeli youth flock to India to deal in drugs and meditation techniques that trivialize the travails of the Israeli people? Is this not a time to evaluate one's relationship to the Almighty? Others, such as the Hasidim retreat to the Wall to recite rote prayers that do not pierce their souls. These live in willful ignorance of the threat to their existence. Is there not a just Judge to be faced at the end of our lifetime? Is there no need to give an account for our thoughts, words, and deeds? Do our lives really have significance in time and eternity? Will our lives stand the trials that will yet come to try our souls?

Does not the kingdom begin in the heart and minds of people before it can ever be expressed in a material and external kingdom? The reason many Jews reject Jesus as the Messiah is because He did not establish an external Maccabean-style kingdom. Yet he clearly asserted that His kingdom was not of this world (John 18:36). The kingdom that broke in pieces the Roman Empire is described by Daniel as a kingdom cut out of the mountains without external help and shall stand forever (Daniel 2:35, 45). To the Son of Man:

"was given dominion and glory and a kingdom that all peoples, nations, and languages should serve him. His dominion is an everlasting dominion, which shall not pass away, and his kingdom the one which shall not be destroyed." (Daniel 7:14)

Is the promise to King David in II Samuel 7:12-13 where the Almighty, the Name, promises *"I will establish his kingdom. . . I will establish the throne of his kingdom forever"* only an external kingdom of land, buildings, elections, and treaties to protect that kingdom? Could the promise of a kingdom be fulfilled by one who rules as king in the hearts and minds of his people? Is not this kingdom a mystery (Matt 3:11) that requires special eyes to see (Matt 13:14)? The kingdom comes not with observation (Luke 17:20) but the kingdom is spiritual requiring that its citizens be poor in spirit, mourners, meek, merciful, pure in heart and peacemakers. The kingdom is evidenced in righteousness which is to be sought at all cost (Matt 5:20 and 6:33). Only being born by the Almighty can qualify a person to enter into the kingdom (John 3:3) *". . . unless one is born of water and the Spirit, he cannot enter the kingdom of God"* (John 3:5).

What is the kingdom? Is it real estate, governmental systems or political process? Is not a kingdom or a state, first and foremost, a moral and spiritual vision? Do the leaders of the state of Israel have such a moral vision? More importantly, do the Jewish people have a moral vision for themselves and for the world for which they are to serve as light? Has not the nation descended into corrupt politics and the youth of the nation increasingly sought escapism into drugs, violence, and degradation? Can any nation exist without a sufficient moral basis?

Jesus as King pierces the conscience with questions that must be faced if you will survive personally or the nation as now constituted will survive collectively.

"Repent for the kingdom of heaven is at hand."
Listen to me, you stubborn hearted, who are far from

105

righteousness: I bring my righteousness near, it shall not be far off; my salvation shall linger, and I will place my salvation in Zion, for Israel My glory." (Isaiah 46:12-13)

This appeal is not based on the ancient rabbinical view that thousands of acts of righteousness (Mitzvot) will usher in the kingdom. In Judaism, the Jewish people are taught that they are required to produce the kingdom. But the Bible teaches that the kingdom is God's accomplishment through the death of Jesus as Messiah on a Roman cross and the Almighty's resurrecting Him from the dead. A revolution in thinking is required to see that the kingdom does not come because of millions of acts of sinful men or in the gradual progress of civilization but the eternal kingdom is completely based on one redemptive act by an eternal person who is both equal to the Almighty in power and glory and could satisfy divine justice. The wages of sin is only paid through death.

Judaistic faith has always looked for a Savior from external problems, not salvation from personal sin and condemnation. The Bible's teaching of the kingdom is both individualistic and non-political. Faith in a personal God who acts out of His own rich mercy in His Son is foundational to the Bible's teaching on the kingdom of God. Biblical faith results in a warm personal relationship with the Almighty. The cross of Jesus has ended the power and influence of this age on one's life so that we might enter the kingdom that will never end. The believer in Jesus is cut loose from this world and lives in the power of the next world.

The kingdom of David's Son who would rule eternally is one lived in the power and hope of that eternal kingdom. Salvation is viewed not from terrorists or oppression but is a present experience not dependent on our temporal circumstances or human effort but on the final work of Jesus the Messiah. The freedom of the Son of David is moral freedom and self-control to live in righteousness without fear all of one's days. This hope is future and includes a resurrection of our bodies and the Savior's changing our body so that we will not experience tears, sorrow or death (Rev 21:4). *"And God will wipe away every tear from their eyes; these shall be no more death, nor sorrow, nor crying. There shall be no more pain, for the former things have passed away."* We are a new creation in Christ according to II Corinthians 5:17. There has been created a totally new environment, or, more accurately speaking, a totally new world, in which the believer is an inhabitant and participator. The deliverance of the created world from the bondage of God's curse is still future but yet the believer can look forward to being delivered from the vanity of this life. We are saved in this hope of the resurrection and the regeneration of the world (Romans 8:18-24). The resurrection of Israel from being a dead branch to a living branch grafted back into the olive tree is a sign of the last days: *"For if their being cast away is the reconciling of the world, what will their acceptance be but life from dead?"* (Rom 11:15). The resurrection is not merely individualistic but includes the revival of God's people so that *"all Israel will be saved,"* the resurrection of the just and the unjust and the renewal of the universe under the Lordship of Jesus Christ (Ephesians 1:10; Philippians 2:10-11).

The work of Jesus in His death and resurrection so establishes the eternal kingdom that no longer is righteousness determined by credit and debit changing day by day. The God of Abraham, Isaac, and Jacob promises forgiveness of sins. Justification before the Almighty is a last judgment anticipated when we know ahead of time we are accepted by the just Judge who is our Savior. He is the Almighty who accepts us as absolutely righteous based on the righteousness fulfilled for us by the Messiah. *"Who shall bring a charge against God's elect? It is God who justifies"* (Romans 8:33). Such a statement is as absolute as the Almighty's sentence of the final judgment. It is so absolute as to be indifferent to the categories of past, present, and future.

The Almighty sends the Spirit on the basis of the work of the Messiah to open blind eyes to honor the Son and receive forgiveness of sins and eternal life. The Spirit is the one who transforms the present life of the believer so that the Messiah's kingdom is experienced in this world. *"The fruit of the Spirit is love, joy, peace, patience, kindness, goodness, faithfulness, gentleness, and self-control"* (Gal 5:22-23). The kingdom is not eating and drinking but righteousness peace and joy in the Holy Spirit. The Spirit is the Messiah in you the hope of glory" (Col 1:27).

In the first century, this message was received by many Jewish people. On the Day of Pentecost, three-thousand believed in Jesus and were baptized on Solomon's Porch on the stairs of the Temple. As a consequence, these Jewish believers continued daily in spiritual unity in the Temple *". . . praising God and having favor with all the people. And the Lord added to the church daily those who were being saved"* (Acts 2:46-47). Five thousand believed as a result of Peter and John's witness in the Temple (Acts 4:4). After the ordination of the first deacons in Acts 6:1-6, the testimony of the Scripture is, *"Then the word of God spread, and the number of the disciples multiplied greatly in Jerusalem, and a great many of the priests were obedient to the faith"* (Acts 4:7).

God has linked Jews and believing Gentiles together. The Church is to include Jews and Gentiles and will never be complete without our joining together in worship of the Messiah and submission to Messiah's rule. Please turn to hear the God of Abraham, Isaac and Jacob.

"Come now, and let us reason together," says the LORD, though your sins are like scarlet, they shall be as white as snow; though they are red like crimson, they shall be as wool. If you are willing and obedient, you shall eat the good of the land; but if

you refuse and rebel, you shall be devoured by the sword"; for the mouth of the LORD has spoken. (Isaiah 1:18-20)

"Seek the LORD while He may be found, call upon Him while He is near. Let the wicked forsake His way and the unrighteous man his thoughts; let him return to the Lord and He will have mercy on him; and to our God, for He will abundantly pardon." (Isaiah 55:6-7)

The Almighty has linked the Church and Jewish people together throughout the centuries.

At the present time, the majority of Jewish people resist the Church and its message. Yet in our covenantal relationship together, the Church and Israel, though standing apart for now with regard to Jesus as the Messiah and Son of God, yet stand together. As the Church, we will never be complete until Jewish people receive their Messiah. In that day, the Almighty One will heal us both and unite us as a witness to the nations of the earth. Please receive the Almighty's forgiveness and cleansing that we might worship as one people. The whole earth waits for your repentance and faith in your Messiah. *"Repent for the kingdom of heaven is at hand."* Enter into the righteousness, peace, and joy of the Messiah's kingdom.

NOTES

Chapter 3

1. Oskar Skarsaune, <u>In the Shadow of the Temple: Jewish Influences on Early Christianity</u>, (Downers Grove, IL: InterVarsity Press, 2002), 262-263.

2. "Profession of Faith, from the Church of Constantinople: From Assemani," Cod. Lit., 105.

3. Abram L. Sachar, <u>A History of the Jews</u>, (Knopf, 1971).

4. David Rausch, <u>A Legacy of Hatred</u>, (Moody Bible Institute of Chicago, 1984), 29.

5. Paul Hilberg, <u>The Destruction of the European Jews</u>

6. Stan Telchin, <u>Abandoned</u>, (Chosen Books, Grand Rapids, MI), 100.

7. Arthur Kac, <u>The Messiahship of Jesus</u>, (Baker Book House, 1986), 140.

Chapter 4

1. Robert Haldane, <u>Exposition of the Epistle to the Romans</u>, (NY Robert Carter, 1847), 551-552.

2. Yoram Hazony, <u>The Jewish State: The Struggle for Israel's Soul</u>, (Basic Books, New York, NY, 2000), 102.

3. John Calvin, <u>Commentaries on the Epistle of Paul the Apostle to the Romans</u>, (W. B. Eerdmans Publishing, Grand Rapids, Michigan, 1959).

Chapter 5

1. Barbara Tuchman, 124.

2. Ibid, 121

3. Ibid, 132

4. Hugh J. Schonfield, <u>The History of Jewish Christianity</u>, (Kemp Hall Press, Ltd. 1936), 209.

5. Biographies of Eminent Hebrew Christians, Gidney, No. IV.

6. Schonfield, 213.

7. Schonfield, 229.

8. Schonfield, 238

Chapter 6

1. <u>O Jerusalem</u>, 357-359.